# FACES & PLACES

## Clonmel 1955-'60

*Justin Nelson*

*Editor*:
Justin Nelson


*Cover Design*:
Don Farrell


ISBN  1 900913 00 3  (Hardback)
      1 900913 01 1  (Paperback)


*Printed by*:
Kilkenny People Printing Ltd.,
34 High Street,
Kilkenny.

A CIP catalogue record for this book is available from the British Library.

First Published in Hardback and Paperback May 1996.
Reprinted June 1996.


Publisher:  Justin Nelson Productions Ltd., Foxrock Park, Dublin 18.

# Preface

Compiling this book was really a labour of love, as it recalled for me so many happy days with *The Nationalist* in the late 1950's. Since then I have never lost touch with Clonmel and South Tipperary during all of my hectic years with RTE, and was glad to feature the area on TV at every possible opportunity.

With RTE, I chose to feature the area in one of the earliest "*Faces & Places*" TV programmes with Kathleen Watkins . . . brought the first show in the Big Top TV series to the Clonmel Showgrounds (featuring among others Linda Martin, just days after her victory in the Eurovision Song Contest) . . . produced an entire *Bibi Show* on Frank Patterson and the St. Mary's Choral Society, as well as being instrumental in setting up the *Nissan Cycling Classic* with it's memorable Sean Kelly time trial from Carrick-on-Suir into Clonmel.

During the '80s it was my pleasure, when John Ryan and Brendan O'Mahoney of the *Clonmel Express* launched the *Clonmel Person of the Year* Awards, to present the award in my name to deserving winners like Mick Delahunty and Tommy O'Brien – both of whom naturally feature in this book.

I wish to thank my former colleague Sean Boland, now Managing Director of *The Nationalist*, who readily gave me permission to use the paper's **copyright** photos and newspaper cuttings in this publication. Sadly many of those featured who were dear friends are no longer with us, but it is my hope that future generations will enjoy this record of their parents and grandparents in the years to come.

My sincere thanks also to my journalistic colleagues of that time for their memories, and especially to the Ceann Comhairle Sean Treacy for his most flattering foreword.

In the main, I have refrained from listing names of those featured in the hundreds of photographs, as I feel it will provide many an enjoyable hour for those who remember the era to recall the thousands of faces contained within these pages. In regard to the dance groups especially – these photos were just a moment in time, so younger readers should not be surprised at seeing Dad with a dance partner other than Mum – or vice versa!

My hope is that this book will recall nothing but happy memories of Golden days .

**OIFIG AN CHEANN COMHAIRLE**
(OFFICE OF CHAIRMAN OF DÁIL ÉIREANN)

**TEACH LAIGHEAN**
(LEINSTER HOUSE)

**BAILE ÁTHA CLIATH 2**
(DUBLIN 2)

I regard it as a source of great pride and joy to be associated with this Treasure House of wonderful pictures taken by Justin Nelson.

It represents a Kaleidoscope of many of the great events and personalities of our time in the 50s which will doubtless bring back in graphic detail a thousand memories, some sad and tragic, some joyous and entertaining. Great characters and old friends emerging throughout the pages, some happily still with us, others sadly gone to their eternal reward.

This wonderful compilation of pictures will, I believe prove most interesting and will tug at the heartstrings of very large numbers of individuals, families, friends and relations who are so graphically depicted in it. Justin Nelson has left us a wonderful legacy of his artistry. I believe it will prove to be a rare keepsake for the vast numbers of our people at home and abroad. A treasure Chest of memories of great events and great people.

We remember the shy, unassuming, immensely popular young man who spent his formative years with us in Clonmel. He was then chosen to join RTE in it's early days where his talents were quickly recognised and he went on to attain the highest TV production position with the RTE Authority, that of Executive Producer, helping to project the nation's great events, many of which involved worldwide coverage such as the visit of the late President John F. Kennedy, the funeral of the late President, Eamon deValera and the visit of His Holiness Pope John Paul 2nd. to Ireland in 1979. He also had the rare distinction of covering some 18 consecutive All Ireland Finals, as well as being in charge of the first ever live colour outside broadcast in Ireland for RTE.

Justin and I met recently in my Office as Chairman of Dail Eireann and as we perused the wonderful array of photographs, it became for us a deeply moving experience so full of poignant memories. One photograph was of particular interest to me. I remember the occasion very well.

My Election Address was ready for printing and a photograph was required urgently. It was during lunch hour that I dashed into Justin's Office to have a few shots taken before going back to work. I have always regarded this photograph as being the real launch of my Public Career.

Little did we think on that day in 1957 that we would meet again almost 40 years later respectively as Ceann Comhairle of Dail Eireann and former Executive Producer of Radio Telefis Eireann. Despite the adversity of the times we lived through, when jobs were scarce and so many of our friends had to take the Emigrant Ship and indeed there was, all around us, evidence of widespread insecurity and social deprivation.

But we were young, we had idealism, we harboured high hopes and ambitions. We had a Dream, - we followed that Dream unrelentingly and lo the Dream came through, Buideacas le Dia.

Thanks for the memories, Justin.

Sean Treacy, T.D.,
Ceann Comhairle.
(Chairman of the Irish House of Representatives)

ABOVE: *Ceann Comhairle Sean Treacy shares a joke with U.S. President Bill Clinton in Dáil Éireann, before inviting him to address both houses of the Oireachtas.*

LEFT: *Photograph I took for the Ceann Comhairle's first General Election campaign, which began his national political career.*

FAR LEFT: *Wearing the historic Mayoral chain during one of his terms as First Citizen of Clonmel.*

*Fair Day in O'Connell Street, Clonmel*

9

Film Stars All! The happy An Óige cast of my "Mountain Magic" film, shot in the Comeraghs.

Mick Del. is joined on the Collins Hall bandstand by Mayor Jim Taylor with the "Mr. Personality" of the 1956 Printers Dance . . . Jimmy O'Dea.

LEFT: Ernie Hogan, as Deputy Mayor, welcomes President Sean T. O'Kelly with Richard Mulcahy T.D. at a Cumann Gaolach dinner.

ABOVE: Mayor Sean Treacy greets Minister for Defence Kevin Boland.

Long before the professional staging of an Árd Feis in the RDS, Eamon de Valera addresses the faithful from a canvas covered lorry outside the Clonmel Town Hall.

Did the telephone callers in South Tipperary realise what lovely ladies answered their calls at Clonmel Post Office?

FANCY DRESS TIME

15

LEFT: Woolworth's staff, about to set off on their annual outing from the store in O'Connell Street.

RIGHT: One of the girls in Kilcoran Lodge rang me to say that Hollywood Star Gene Kelly was a resident, but for Heaven's sake not to mention the source of my information! When I introduced myself, he was so helpful, and offered to show his new Irish boots to two of the staff, and so make a nice picture for me.

His "Singing in the Rain" routine is now a classic. I took the photo (below) of him with Debbie Reynolds from the TV screen when the movie was shown yet again to mark his death in 1996.

Happy Féile Cluain Meala winners.

When taking this picture of my press colleagues before an All-Ireland Final in Croke Park (in pre-Hogan Stand days), I could hardly have imagined that within a decade I would be in charge of the TV coverage in these much changed grounds for the first of 18 consecutive years of All-Ireland Football Finals.

*For the girls in my life,*
*Loretto, Aisling,*
Niamh and Tara

# CONTENTS

# When Dreams Come Through

## Justin Nelson

My 1950 *classmates in Summerhill College, Sligo – where many successful careers began.*

It was early in October 1955 and I had just begun my second year in College in Dublin. Perhaps my career was about to take a new turn. The old steam train down from Dublin was cold and poorly lit - on this, my first journey to Clonmel. The only other passenger in the railway carriage trundling along in the Winter darkness through Horse and Jockey, Farnaleen and Fethard suggested I'd best spend the night in a B&B near the Railway Station. There was quite a walk down to the town, he told me, and as I was in a strange new environment on a dark frosty night, I took his advice. My first over-night in Clonmel would be spent over the Spanish Arms pub up beside the Railway Station. What was I doing here in this strange town, where the smell of crushed apples was everywhere?

From the time I was about 10 years old, my future career was well defined - in my own mind at least! Later, coming towards the Leaving Cert. in Summerhill College in Sligo, Bishop Hanley, on one of his regular visits would enquire if we - pupils of this Diocesan College - had made up our minds on what we proposed to do with ourselves after finishing College.

Fellow students of the time like future Taoiseach Albert Reynolds might well have said, "I'm going to make a fortune - running dance halls and manufacturing cat food", while the future EC commissioner, young Ray McSharry would leave shortly to help his uncle, the cattle dealer. Others were about to begin outstanding careers in medicine, banking and engineering, as well as in the Church.

"Yes, I know what I'm going to do" was the reply when my turn came. He was delighted and enquired no further, for here was the probability of yet another young man heading for the priesthood in Maynooth. Bishop Hanley was not to know that one day this particular student had ambitions to make movies no less - like maybe, "*The Great Caruso*", or even "*The Ten Commandments*" which he had seen down in the Gaiety Cinema in Sligo! Though he never quite reached the Hollywood heights, he would still fulfil most of his ambitions during 34 wonderfully exciting years as a TV Producer with RTE television, which was not even a dream in most people's imagination at this time.

The seeds of my future career were sown away back around 1927, when John Logie Baird first invented televison. The image of a ventriloquist's dummy had been succesfully transmitted accross a room.

My far seeing Co. Leitrim school master father had bought a few shares in the Baird company before I had ever seen the light of day. However, when the Logie Baird TV system was not adopted by the BBC in it's first experimental transmissions in 1936, my future career (possibly in the manufacture of TV transmission systems) took a crushing blow ! The company was taken over by the mighty J. Arthur Rank Organisation, and all of the original shareholders, including my dad, became part of one of the world's biggest film production companies of the time. For me, this was perhaps a blessing in disguise, for I would eagerly await the huge glossy annual report sent to shareholders. As the huge circular gong was banged by the sweating bare chested strongman in the opening titles of each new J. Arthur Rank film, I was certain this was the business for me.

Until I could rise to the cost of a movie camera, I had to settle for the family Kodak Box Brownie! My bedroom window would be blocked up with the quilt from the bed, while the airless room stank with the smell of developer and fixer chemicals, as I produced contact prints of my youthful photographic endeavours. My other passion at the time was making radios, and my speciality was making headphones from the most basic of items - like lenghts of wire coiled around sawn off six inch nails with razor blades being one of the main components!

This was the era long before Hi-Fi and the Walkmans. I would listen to the excitement of Michael O'Hehir's Gaelic games commentaries each Sunday afternoon - little realising that in later life we would not only become firm friends, but I would have the honour of being in charge of the TV coverage with him of 18 consecutive All-Ireland finals which would be relayed live by satellite to the four corners of the world, as well as exciting race meetings at the Curragh and elsewhere.

So with the Leaving Cert. done, it was natural that I would head off to do radio engineering in Dublin (with the hope of a job eventually in Radio Éireann), while at the same time attending night classes in photography in the North Strand Tech. This was the era when cycling across the city one had to be careful not to come a cropper in the narrow tram tracks still on the city streets. Home to Sligo for the weekend, my mother showed me an advertisement in the *Irish Independent* from a newspaper in Clonmel looking for a staff photographer. This would fulfil one side of my ambitions, but what did I have to show of my photograpic skills?. This was a period of great unemployment in Ireland, with thousands emigrating to find work wherever one could find it,- on the shores of Amerikay, or on the building sites in London.

I was one of the lucky ones, for my application must have impressed, and now I was about to attend an interview here in Clonmel for the first job application I had ever made. I had made my way down through Prior Park to Market Street, and rather timidly entered the Nationalist Office. It was just 10 am, and as I was soon to find out, the Editor, Mr. W.C. Darmody would by now be down in the Friary attending his daily Mass. This routine, through Winter and Summer, irrespective of whatever crisis might arise, would never be broken throughout his good life.

A large man with a ready smile, he instantly made me feel at ease. Soon he would be joined by the paper's senior editorial staff Brendan Long, who was later to succeed him as editor, and Edmond Symes who went on to become Editor of Dáil debates, and has contributed an interesting piece on the cinemas and theatres of Clonmel for this publication. Edmond was a keen photographer, and was there to query my knowledge of pho-tography. Later still, the Chairman of the board of Directors Mr. T.K. Murphy called up from his business in O'Connell St. to vet this new recruit.

Fr. Cyril O.F.M.

Before the morning was out the Editor brought in his dear friend (and mine too for the succeeding years and the celebrant at my wedding years later), Fr. Cyril from the Franciscan Friary. I must have passed all of their tests, for I was offered the job.

Even though my parents had already paid my college fees for the term, I just announced to them that I had got myself a job, and would be starting shortly. They never queried my decision, or enquired what sort of career this was going to provide in return for all the hard earned money they had spent on my education. Incidentally, several years later when I had become a TV producer, I received a nice letter of congratulation from Bishop Hanley (whom I have mentioned above) wishing me every success - so the fact that this Summerhill College pupil never made it to Maynooth was forgiven !

Even in the surroundings of The Nationalist printing works there was always time for a laugh and a celebration with colleagues, for the smallest of reasons. This was the era of hot metal type, but the foretaste of future printing methods was indicated by the Klishograph engraving machine which I operated, seen being serviced (on right) by a German Engineer. My knowledge of electronics often proved useful when faults developed.

Some years after joining *The Nationalist*, I was flattered, to be told by the Editor, Mr. Darmody that from the moment I had entered his office he knew their quest was over. My knowledge of electonics was a further plus in my CV, for the company was about to install the country's first electonic engraving machine, and this would form part of my job specification. Up until this time the metal engravings which were used to transfer the photographic image on to the printed page was carried out by a method which involved a photographic process using acid to cut into a metal plate. This process would now be done by a machine developed and manufactured in Germany, called the Klishograph, which would scan the photograph by means of a tiny beam of light.

This in turn would control a stylus cutting into a hard plastic plate, and thus etch out the image which would be inserted amongst the lead type to make up the printed page. Not only would the Nationalist be the first Provincial newspaper in Ireland to use this system, but the Dublin dailies were soon to follow our lead. So began the first steps on a career which over the past 40 years has fulfilled all of my youthful ambitions, and many more besides. When I joined the Nationalist staff I was just 20 years of age, and with school days over, life was really great.

On my arrival in Clonmel to begin work, Brendan Long not only recommended an

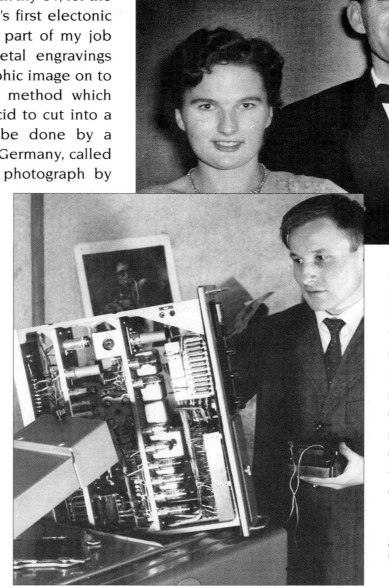

excellent lodgings for me in "Melrose" on Powerstown Rd., but with his girlfriend Ina invited me to join them in a visit to the Ritz Cinema on my first night in Clonmel. I was quickly made feel at home. The film was a Western, but shortly I'd be watching Bill Haley and the Comets in "Rock around the Clock" in this same cinema, which now houses the Clonmel Credit Union. What a time it was to have a steady job and not a care in the world!

ABOVE: *Senior reporter and later Editor, Brendan Long with his sister Pat, and his wife to be Ina.*

Just a few months earlier, the new weekly *Munster Tribune* had begun publication in the town. This could have caused severe competition for *The Nationalist*, which had been around for several generations, and at that time carried advertising on its front cover. *The Tribune* had set new standards in newspaper design in the region, and featured a considerable amount of photographs which were a rarity in the Provincial Press of the time. In fact, were it not for the arrival of this competition in the local newspaper field, it is doubtful if the Directors of *The Nationalist* would have gone to the extra expense of hiring their own staff photographer. A young man by the name of Tommy Carey was the *Tribune's* "Strolling Photographer" as he was called.

On my first day of employment in Clonmel, the Editor suggested I take a stroll down by the Suir to get to know the town a little better, or maybe he thought the tranquility of the scene along the river bank would help me settle in to this, for me, strange environment. Near the gashouse bridge I found two workmen taking readings from a gadget out in the middle of the river. As I was now a real "newshound", I thought I should enquire what they were doing, while getting them to pose for my camera.

## They're Doing Something About Suir Drainage !

Alderman Senator Denis E. Burke, Mayor of Clonmel, advocated at a County Council meeting this week, that all year round work could be provided for a permanent staff if a system of alternating road work with drainage work could be adopted.

When he made this suggestion, Ald. J.J. Morrissey commented that the problem was what were the men going to clean rivers and streams into.

"They turned down the Anner", he said, "because the River Suir can't take it. You would'nt be allowed to do this kind of work because it is out of the question until the arterial drainage scheme is carried out of the river Suir"

How long the farmers of the county will have to wait for this vitally necessary and major job to be done remains a matter for conjecture, but Justin Nelson, "The Nationalist " Staff Photographer, strolling by the Suir at Clonmel early this week came upon technicians of the engineering branch of the Board of Works, who were determining the amount of drainage that is required.

The men who were doing this highly technical job were Mr. H.D.Shine and Mr. Pierce Butler. Measurements were carried out by means of an instrument which records the speed at which the water flows. It is lowered into the water at various distances from the bank. A wheel which is located on the top is rotated by the water and each complete revolution is signalled on earphones at two feet per second.

Our first picture shows Mr. Shine using earphones to receive rotation signals and making his calculations. second picture is of the instrument itself.

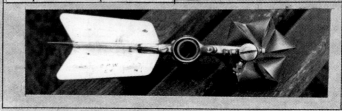

The resulting couple of pictures introduced me to the readers with an item which proclaimed that at last they were doing something about draining the Suir. Perhaps an election was in the offing, for in those days each political party would make firm promises to drain the Shannon when elected. Now with the devastation caused by the flooding along the quays in 1996 the much needed work, which we thought in 1955 was about to take place, has yet to begin!

Soon, I had got the hang of this new career, helped initially in no small way by the two established photographers in the town - the late Willie Boland, and Michael Keating. Both made me most welcome, even though I was now taking away a source of their own incomes. Willie Boland's studio was in part of *The Nationalist's* buildings in Market St., while Michael , or M.A. Keating as he was known, was down in Nelson St. beside the Courthouse.

Michael always had the latest camera equipment the moment it came on the market, and experimented with colour photography when it was a real novelty. Both did a good business in weddings, confirmations, and First Holy Communion portraits, while Willie also specialised in Gaelic games team pictures at every level from club to county. For many years Michael's assistant was Ralph - nobody ever seemed to know his surname. When things would not be busy up at The

*Nationalist*, I would always be welcome for a chat in their darkroom down in Nelson St. where we could "talk shop".

I was accepted into membership of the National Union of Journalists, and in my first few weeks was paid at the lower rate appropriate for my young years. However, as part of my duties included the operation of the Klishograph engraving machine, a sort of union job demarcation dispute soon reared its head, as often happens with the introduction of new technology. In order to work as an engraver, one had to be a member of SLADE, which was the trade union representing lithographers, artists,designers, and engravers. To settle this inter-union dispute, the NUJ agreed that yes I should become a member of SLADE, but however they would kindly pay my annual union subscription for me! So, not only was I now to become a member of a very closed and difficult to enter trade union, but a further union complication was to be to my great advantage. It appears, a junior member of the NUJ could not be allowed do this reasonably technical engraving work, so what was the solution? The company could either employ a further senior staff member to do the work, or I would have to become a full NUJ member and in the process get paid the top journalist rate by T*he Nationalist*. To my eternal gratitude, the company agreed to this very satisfactory arrangement from my point of view, whatever about their thoughts on the demerits of this sort of plan!

The Directors of *The Nationalist* at the time included Senator D.E. Burke who was also Mayor of Clonmel in 1955, his brother Ulick, Michael White who had a spirit store in Gladstone St., Edward Beary who was the County Registrar and Returning Officer at election times, Anthony Murphy who had a grocery, wine and spirits business in O'Connell St. and John Smyth who was much younger than all of the others, and as far as I know is the only living survivor at this time. The Company Secretary was J.V. Dillon, whose son Ted was on the reporting staff.

FAR LEFT: When Senator D. E. Burke's daughter Valerie celebrated her 21st birthday, I of course went along to the party held at Raheen.

LEFT: Some of the other guests – such as Tony O'Reilly (who can now afford to pay more than $2 million for Jackie Kennedy's engagement ring), have made quite a name for themselves since.

ABOVE: My family picture of another of the newspaper's Directors – the Murphys pictured at home in Davis Road.

The *Munster Tribune* was printed by the *Sporting Press* down on Davis Rd., and appeared on Thursday evenings. Its first editor was Fintan Faulkner, and the editorial staff included Barney Cavanagh who was later to join me in RTE, Des Mullan who is now Political Correspondent with the *Evening Herald*, Mick Strappe who later joined *The Nationalist* staff, (all of whom have kindly contributed articles for this publication) and the late Michael Hogan. Later the *Munster Tribune* was edited by Raymond Smyth for a short time. Raymond later became one of the country's best known news reporters and covered the big news stories all over the world for the *Irish Independent* group, while at the same time producing an endless stream of books on topics as diverse as sport and gambling, to biographies of Garret Fitzgerald and Charlie Haughey. Some of his memories of Clonmel too are included in this book.

ABOVE: *Adverts on the front page and the Tuesday tabloid size edition.* BELOW: *Tony Houlihan works the Linotype in the Market Street printing works.*

*My reporter colleagues – Front (from left): Des Mullan, Barney Cavanagh, Brendan Long. Back (from left): Ted Dillon, Mick Strappe, Myself (the shy one!), Willie Fenton and Michael Hogan. Sadly Ted, Willie and Michael have since died, R.I.P., but all of the others have written articles for this book.*

In those days, *The Nationalist* produced a tabloid newspaper for the Clonmel area each Tuesday, followed by the main edition on Thursday, which sold in big numbers not only in South Tipperary, but in the adjoining counties of Limerick, Cork, Kilkenny and Waterford. It, like most of the provincial newspapers of the period, carried advertising on its front page. A Clonmel edition of the paper was printed on Saturdays, so we were kept busy right throughout the week. With Sunday being the main news day - particularly from a sports point of view, those of us on the editorial section of the paper often worked all seven days of the week. Present day NUJ members would be horrified at the very idea of such a thing. However, life was very carefree, and I enjoyed every moment of it all. Editor W.C. Darmody never queried the time we arrived in or left the office, so long as the work got done.

Often on a Monday morning he would enquire what functions I had attended over the week-end, and would gladly accept my own choice of events that I had covered for the paper. The company's small Morris van would have been at my disposal, and it was at the expense of its clutch that I first learned to drive! However, I must credit Tom Taylor who owned a hire car in Morton St., and Brian Reidy who was a colleague in the Nationalist at that time as my driving instructors. There were no driving tests in those days.

I was just a couple of months in the job when, early on Thursday morning 22nd December 1955, a major story broke in our circulation area. As our new electronic engraving machine had been installed just a few days previously, we were now in a position to offer a very fast reproduction of pictures of a late story. Normally, I would hear the fire brigade siren (which summoned the part-time staff) when it sounded during the night. My landlady at the time Mrs O'Brien, in "Melrose", Powerstown Rd., had lived through the war years in London, and would always awaken to the sound of the siren even if I didn't. I would dash off to the fire station up near the Garda Barracks, usually arriving on my Lambretta scooter as quickly as some of the fire brigade staff, who would come dashing in from all over the town.

*A scooter blessing by Fr. Cyril at the Friary.*

If it was anything more than a chimney fire, I would go off and take a photograph of the blaze. I developed a good relationship with the lads on the fire crew, and on a number of occasions I feel was allowed time to capture my blazing shot, before it would be all "ruined" from my point of view, by being doused with the water hoses!

Fires at McCreery's shop in O'Connell Street and at the Railway Station. Occasionally, I got to the scene before the brigade!

Anyway, on this particular night I must have slept soundly, for it was not 'till I arrived in to the office around 9 o'clock, that the senior reporter Edmond Symes, (who was later to become editor of the Dáil debates) told me about a train crash which had happened during the night out at Cahir. Apparently a heavily loaded sugar-beet special, running from Wexford via Limerick Junction to Thurles was running several hours late when it arrived into Cahir Station. The night mail was already in the station loading mail, so the beet special was switched into a siding, and the "home" signal about three quarters of a mile from the station was signalled to stop the oncoming train. However, instead of slowing down, the train gathered speed with the train driver blowing the whistle while entering the station at 30 miles an hour. The 150 ton loco hit the stop block, and of course crashed through it. There were now no tracks under the onrushing carriages which smashed through the viaduct plunging into the River Suir, taking 22 of the heavily laden wagons with it.

Both the driver and fireman died instantly, and steam was still hissing from the partly submerged engine when I arrived on the scene. It was a gruesome sight, but I quickly took my pictures from a variety of angles and sped back to Clonmel.

On arrival back to the Nationalist Office in Market St., I remember a breathless Editor pacing up and down outside the darkroom, anxiously wondering what I had on film, because by now the layout of the news pages were being finalised. We would be going to press later that afternoon, and the advantage of having our own photo engraving machine would soon become apparent. It is always an anxious time when you load the exposed film into a development tank in total darkness. As you pour in a succession of chemicals to carry out the development process, there is always the danger of using incorrect temperatures when one is

rushed, mistiming the procedure, or horror of horrors reversing the order of the chemicals. Anyway, all was well on this occasion, and the Editor could rest assured that I would come up with dramatic pictures of the scene, so that we could have our paper on the streets before the *Evening Herald* or *Evening Echo* arrived in town. We were ready to start the printing presses on time with five of my photographs on the main news page. Within two months of taking up the job, I had passed my first crucial test.

# Fatal Rail Tragedy At

Some idea of the tangled mass of shattered steel, timber and tons of sugar beet may be had from this picture taken at the scene of the crash by Nationalist Staff Photographer Justin Nelson

### "TRAIN WAS OUT OF CONTROL"
—GUARD

### PROCEEDINGS OF THIS MORNING'S INQUEST

"COMING INTO CAHIR STATION I HAD THE FEELING THAT THE TRAIN WAS OUT OF CONTROL," declared William Grant, who was guard on the beet special which crashed over the River Suir Viaduct at Cahir Station in the early hours of Thursday morning, killing the engine-driver, Cornelius ... and the ... man, Fra... Trahill.

*By using a delay timer on the camera I managed to include myself too in the occasional picture (although not for publication) – like here (centre back) with fellow members of the SS. Peter & Paul's Pioneer Council and (on left) near the top of Ben Nevis in Scotland with some of my Clonmel An Óige colleagues.*

For the most part, the work was fairly stress free, photographing groups attending meetings, dances, Hunt Balls and Socials, the opening of a new school, mayoral receptions down at the Town Hall and such like, forming the day to day content of my photographic assignments. It was a great way for a young stranger in town to get to know lots of people in all walks of life. I found everybody most welcoming, and to this day can bore people with talk of this "town I loved so well". In fact many of my colleagues in RTE think that I am a native of Clonmel.

Being young and single, I quickly got involved in just about every society in the town - from An Óige to the Fencing Club, Cumann Gaolach, Hillview Pitch & Putt, Scooter Club, Film Society, Pioneer Association, and of course attended just about every dance in the Collins Hall.

ABOVE: *Two of my fencing club colleagues, Siobhán Kearney (left) who died sadly as I was assembling this book and Kathleen O'Neill.*

ABOVE RIGHT: A *happily retired Mick Del. as he appeared on screen in my Clonmel "Faces & Places" TV programme.*

This was the Mick Del. era, but also the beginning of Rock and Roll in Ireland with the Clipper Carlton, Brendan Bowyer and the Royal Showband. It was said the Royal were happy to play the Collins Hall for a total fee of £30 a night at this, the start of their career. But soon they would become the Superstars of the period, and can proudly boast that they were top of the bill in the U.K. with an up and coming young group of fellows called "The Beatles" playing in the support role! (In later years I regularly featured Brendan Bowyer on RTE TV shows, and gave his daughter Aisling, who is now an established entertainer in the States, her first appearance on television.)

One of the Directors of the Collins Hall was also on the board of the Nationalist, and this together with the publicity I could generate by having photos of patrons enjoying themselves published in the paper ensured my free admission to all of the dances. I could also rely on getting tickets to the many formal occasions like the Clonmel Harriers and the Tipperary Hunt Balls, Military Ball, Hillview, Island, etc. It could be tricky trying to carry out the work without it interfering unduly with my love life! Suitably attired for the occasion, I would always be one of the first to arrive in the ballroom.

LEFT: *Jacqueline and Vincent O'Brien at the Hunt Ball.*

The idea was to get a few groups of smiling patrons together as early as posible, so that I could then abandon the camera in the office across the road from the Collins Hall, and head off to pick up my own dance partner. It was a sort of Cinderella in reverse as far as she were concerned, as my partner for the night would have to wait patiently in all her glamour at home for me to arrive to take her to the Ball - but at least we always arrived well before the midnight bells had rung! This way, I was able to separate my work from my social life. These dress dances rarely finished before 3 or 4 a.m. anyway, so there was plenty of time for Mick Del's "American Patrol" and "In the Mood"!

Later, I would use my artistic(!) talents to paint a colourful poster each week announcing the coming attraction to the Collins hall, like one of a biggest names in Irish Showbusiness of the time, Bridie Gallagher, or "The Girl from Donegal" as she was known.

Mr. Sweetman, the town's bill poster, would paste up my hand painted poster on the hoarding outside the Hall. For this I would pay him the going rate of 6d, which came out of my weekly fee of seven shillings and six pence (about 37p). However, due to pressure of work, or laziness on my part, there were several occasions when I did not have the "art" work ready when he was doing his rounds sticking up posters on billboards all over the town. I, however, never shirked a job just because it involved getting my hands dirty. So I got the paste and stuck up the poster myself. Soon, my good friend Tony Cantwell, who was the compositor in our printing works, and I suppose the senior trade unionist on the staff, mentioned to me (tongue in cheek) that he had got a complaint from Mr. Sweetman, and was about to notify the "Bill-Posters Union" about my activities! So there was nothing for it, but to call up to the Sweetman home in Peter St., apologise profusely, and solve the situation in a flash by agreeing to pay him the 6d a week which he would have earned for doing the job, but continue pasting up the posters myself! At this stage of my career, I was already a full union member of both the NUJ and SLADE, but I drew the line at joining the Bill-Posters Union as well - even if such a union existed!

It was the normal procedure then - as I presume it still is, that the local journalists supplied the daily papers with reports of the local news. I soon got in on the act myself and would regularly post off a photograph to the Dublin dailies, and when it was used, I would receive the huge payment for those times of a guinea! (About £20 in to-days terms). It supplemented my income without any extra endeavour. In those days the *Sunday Independent* would carry a full back page of photographs, and its famous Editor of the time, Hector Legge became an admirer of my photographic work. He introduced a "Picture of the Week" which took up almost the entire back page. Each Sunday he would choose the photograph, almost always taken by one of the Independent Group photographic staff, but on many occasions he chose one of mine. The Dublin staff photographers would not be pleased that this youth from the country would be chosen ahead of them.

An example of one of my photographs chosen as Picture of the Week is this one which formed more than half the back page of the *Sunday Independent* of December 7th. 1958.

There's excitement now in Cashel,
For the railway soon will run,
There's commotion in the City,
For the line is nearly done,
There's signs and preparations,
That were never seen before,
And the rising generations,
Sees prosperity in store.
　　　- *Francis Phillips*. 1904.

Cashel Railway station had been opened in 1901, but the last passenger train had used the station in 1947. In the following years its only use was for goods transport on the six miles of

branch line to Goold's Cross, but even this too was now being discontinued. My picture showed Mr. John Delaney who had looked after the maintenance of the track and buildings for the previous 43 years, standing in the doorway, while workmen smashed down the structure he had tended so carefully all of those years.

However having one's photograph chosen as Picture of the Week caused a small panic on one occasion. I had now moved "digs" from Powerstown Rd., to Mrs Claire Roche's lovely home, "Bellevue" on the Western Rd., and I remember her anxiously coming into my bedroom early one Sunday morning with a telegram. In those days, telegrams always brought bad news. With sleepy eyes, I fumbled the green envelope open. "HOLDING OVER YOUR PIC TO NEXT WEEK STOP DO NOT SUBMIT IT ELSEWHERE STOP EDITOR SUNDAY INDEPENDENT."

For the Picture of the Week I received a fee of £5, (probably equivalent to £100 in to-day's money) which was great news, in addition to its prestige value. However the photographer's name was never mentioned, so I was to remain unknown!

On the big occasion, like an All-Ireland Hurling Final day, the dailies would have several of their photographic staff covering the event, but luckily my solo efforts on many occasions proved superior. I would always come up with a full page of pictures, sometimes capturing the disputed incident or "talking point" of the match. A good example is my famous picture of Christy Ring and Mick Mackey.

This photograph has followed me all over the world. Last Summer, almost 40 years since I took it, I was making a TV programme in America when a Cork priest says "Didn't you take that famous picture of Christy Ring and Mick Mackey?". All of the national dailies have reprinted it at some stage. It has also appeared in "Ireland of the Welcomes", in Raymond Smyth's "Hurling Immortals", Val Dorgan's book on Christy Ring, on the cover of a sound cassette, will shortly appear in a history of the GAA being written by Cashel author Seamus King and only recently a Dublin PR agency was contemplating using it in a poster campaign.

Years after I had taken it at a Munster Final in Limerick, I had the pleasure of meeting Mick Mackey in connection with a TV programme I was doing on hurling. He jokingly gave out to me for all the years of torment when he had to put up with people asking him - "But what did Ring really say to you that day?" Mackey was a gentle giant of a man, and it was my great pleasure to have been the only person ever to photograph the two greatest names in hurling together. Luck was with me when taking the picture at a Munster Final in Limerick in 1957. Mackey was one of the umpires, who had earlier disallowed a score from Ring, and as the Cork maestro left the pitch following an arm injury they exchanged greetings!

I kept an ever changing display of photos in the Market St. office windows. However, on a few occasions the Editor suggested to me following a comment at that week's Board of Directors meeting, that perhaps the display needed changing.

It was probably just a coincidence that Dev or some other high-ranking Fianna Fáil politician was on display just a little too long for the Chairman, Senator D.E. Burke's liking! The Directors of The Nationalist in those days, (it has since changed ownership), were very strong Fine Gael supporters, but all credit is due to the Editor of the time, W.C. Darmody who maintained a very fair political balance in the news pages.

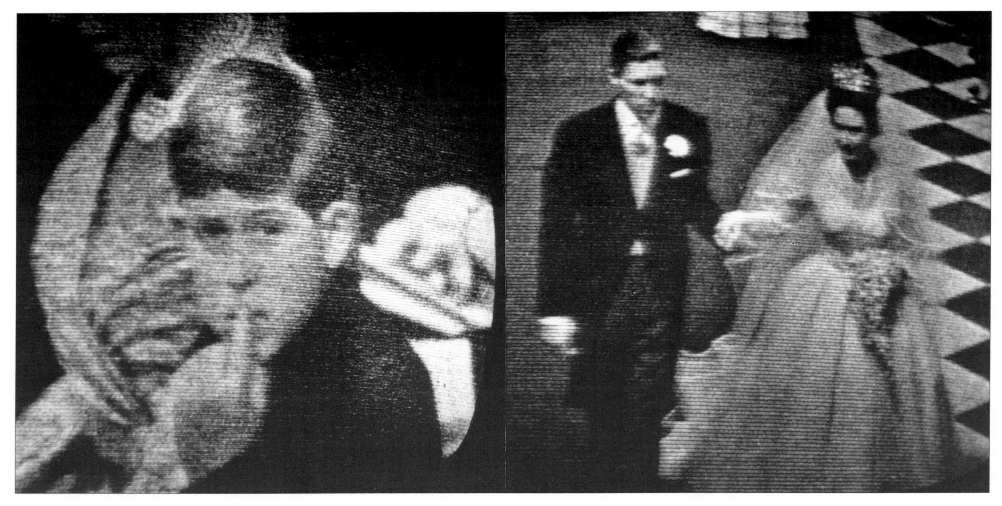

On occasions I would display photographs in the Nationalist windows which at the time may have raised some eyebrows. One such occasion was the Royal wedding of Princess Margaret to Lord Snowden. I felt a particular affinity with his "Lordship" being a photographer - or Tony Armstrong Jones, as he was then. I had heard there was a television set somewhere up around Ballingarane which could receive snowy pictures from a BBC transmitter in Wales.

So on the morning of the wedding, Peggy Hickey from the reporting staff and myself barged in on the family viewing without as much as an invitation. I set up my camera tripod in the prime viewing area in front of the screen and proceeded to capture the spectacular scene in Westminister Abbey. Dashing back to the office, I had huge enlargements of the Royal wedding ceremony on display within ten minutes, all credited to myself.

Whatever about the reaction such a display would have provoked in the original founders of a newspaper called *"The Nationalist"*, it certainly caused great interest- especially to the girls in the Co. Council Office around the corner, when they came out for their lunchtime break. The fact that the pictures were quite fuzzy due to the 405 lines black and white transmission of the time, as well as the poor TV reception, only added to the mystique of the whole operation from my point of view, for it confirmed the impression that I was actually over in London for the wedding and had sent these photos back to Clonmel by wirephoto!

These were happier times for many of the Royal family, especially for the young Prince Charles whom I captured with my camera almost 40 years ago. Later I would be on the tarmac at Shannon airport to photograph the arrival of the Royal newly weds off the Aer Lingus Viscount, when they came to visit relations in Birr Castle.

When the first Russian sputnik was launched, I was out at 6.30 that first morning to photograph it on its first orbit around the world. It was clearly visible to the human eye in the still darkened sky over

Clonmel , but sadly when I peered at the resulting negative I could find no trace of it! There was nothing for it but to do a huge enlargement anyway, and on to it I stuck a big arrow pointing to the largest speck of white on the print. Underneath, the caption said it was the Sputnik. - Well it WAS in there somewhere!

However, taking "still" photographs was all very well, but what about the movies and Hollywood and all that! Maurice Dougan, whose chemist's Shop was in Mitchell St. at the time - knowing my interest in buying a 16mm movie camera, got me some brochures. I had my heart set on the top of the range which was the Paillard-Bolex made with precision engineering in Switzerland. Maurice very kindly offered to forego his own profit margin, so in effect I would be getting it at the wholesale price. I still needed a loan from the bank of the huge sum of £100. I got an interview with the Manager of the Provincial, then situated in what is now the Clonmel Arms. He was somewhat dubious about granting me the loan, perhaps I didn't look like a person who would ever repay it - even though my only brother was on the Provincial Staff. (In fact he was soon to become one of the country's youngest branch managers.) Anyway, the bank eventually granted the loan, and the manager left me feeling he was doing me a special favour. With Maurice Dougan's help, I had become the proud owner of a 16mm movie camera.

However, my mother in Sligo was horrified when she heard I had borrowed money, and insisted she give me the £100, so that I would not be in debt to the bank. It was a sizeable sum in those days - probably the equivalent of £2,000 in to-day's terms. In later years I think she enjoyed my small success in the business which had begun with her help in obtaining that first movie camera. One of her proudest moments involved her presence at Knock Shrine during Pope John Paul's historic visit in 1979. Because I was in charge of the world wide television coverage, I succeeded in getting her over-night accomodation in a third floor bedroom in the convent overlooking the Shrine. One needed to be of Cardinal rank (at least!) to merit such a location, from which she had an uninterupted grand-stand view of the entire ceremony.

Anyway back to Clonmel of the late fifties. Around this time, the Clonmel Film Society was very active, with regular showings in the Regal Theatre, and I got to be a member of the committee. I was also an active member of An Óige - so here was the ideal combination through which I could progress my moviemaking.

What a wonderfully happy group we were. The outcome was a 13 minute colour film, to which Brendan Long, who was chairman of the Film Society, added a commentary. But how were we to show it to the public, while at the same time recouping some of the funds used in its making.? There were Revenue Commissioners restrictions over the public showing of films, but surely we couldn't be prevented from "inviting" our friends along to see the Premiere in the Regal Theatre down on Davis Rd.? A leading light in An Óige was my friend Aidan Kilkelly who recalls our wonderful days hiking in the Comeraghs later in this book. His father, Mick was Mayor of Clonmel that year. Once the Mayor would attend in his full mayoral robes, the performance had a certain prestige value, so that lots of townspeople would also wish to come along. In the event, almost 700 people packed out the Regal Theatre. We proudly watched the curtains go back and the "Mountain Majic" opening credits rolled, and if each member of the public absolutely insisted on giving a donation of half a crown to An Óige in return for the invitation it seemed rude to refuse! It might not be "Ben Hur", but for me, all my boyhood dreams seemed at last to be coming through.

With not even a mention yet of an Irish TV service, I contacted both the BBC and ITN in London to offer my services as a freelance newsreel cameraman in Ireland. Soon I would cover a number of major news stories on their behalf, the most spectacular being the ill-fated Alitalia Plane crash at Shannon. It was an eerie sight, as my picture clearly illustrates.

Around this time too, I got involved in the making of a film on the Rock of Cashel with Joe Irwin, Michael Burke and I recall a very photogenic Vera McGovern being our leading lady. While shot mainly on, or around the famous rock, I recall a quite hilarious moment in the filming which involved Michael Burke having to fall out of a boat into the lake at Rockwell College.

The film's subsequent acceptance for showing at the Cork Film Festival, in theory sounds impressive, but the actual event itself proved an absolute fiasco, when the projectionist ran the film at the wrong speed, giving it a Charlie Chaplin comedy appearance. The same festival also included another short film I had made in Donegal. I also recall filming the "stand -down" or final parade through Clonmel of the 13th infantry battalion from Kickham Barracks, and its subsequent screening in the Regal Theatre as part of the Clonmel Film Society programme.

These references, together with the help of my good friend, Travel Agent Pat Rafferty got me the exciting task of filming the history making inaugural Aer Lingus Boeing 707 jet flight from Shannon to New York, which replaced the slow flying propeller driven Constellation planes which lumbered across the Atlantic at little more than a couple of hundred miles an hour.

In subsequent years with RTE, I've been fortunate to travel all over the world to such exciting spots as the Bahamas, Hong Kong,

New Zealand, Hawaii, Australia, Key Biscayne, Israel, Moscow etc., but the thrill of that history making first jet flight across the Atlantic has remained with me. It was in the month of March, and Idlewild Airport in New York was snow bound, so we were diverted to Halifax, Nova Scotia. The following day we were able to take off again for the Big Apple, and I recall the splendour of New York's Waldorf Astoria where we had a superb banquet, courtesy of Aer Lingus.

I remained on in New York to cover the St. Patrick's day parade down Fifth Avenue for the *Sunday Independent*, which carried a complete back page of my pictures two days later. In order to process the Parade pictures before heading out to Idlewild Airport to put them on a flight back to Ireland I had to close myself into the wardrobe in my hotel bedroom to ensure complete darkness! - Just as well I didn't suffer from claustrophobia. I also recall watching the famous Ed. Sullivan Show on television in my hotel room, and the performance of a group of Aran jumper clad brothers from Carrick-on-Suir which I had never heard of before. Later, it would be my pleasure to feature the same Clancy Brothers on many a TV show of my own.

And so it came to 1961 when Radio Éireann began advertising for trainee staff for the, soon to be launced, new television service - Telefis Éireann. Whereas I could have happily settled for a much more carefree and less nervewrecking life in Clonmel, this opportunity was too good to let pass, and one which, if I were successful, would keep me on my planned career path. My filming achievements, together with the experience I had gained during my years in Clonmel had obviously impressed the recruitment panel, and I was fortunate to become one of the 24 selected as the first batch of recruits from the thousands who had applied. My boyhood ambitions were about to be realised.

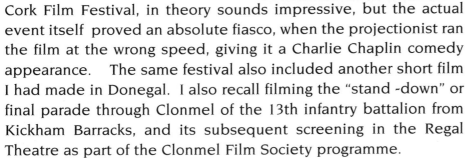

Coverage of the President John F. Kennedy visit to Ireland so soon after the launch of RTE was a major undertaking. From my vantage point on the control tower at Dublin Airport (below right), it was my proud duty to relay the historic arrival of Air Force One - not only to viewers in Ireland but via the Early Bird Satellite around the world.

By sheer coincidence my very last day as a TV cameraman was to be in the Regal Theatre in Clonmel where we were recording a programme in 1963. With me are colleagues Aidan Maguire and Tom Fawcett.

Religion played a major part in 50s life. LEFT: The close of the Mission in
SS. Peter & Paul's and (above and right) The May Procession packed Gladstone Street
right down to the Main Guard.

*The men also turned out in force for the Corpus Christi Procession.*

*The missing Ormonde Hotel is but one example of how Gladstone Street has changed in the intervening years.*

Chipperfield's Circus arrived in force at Clonmel Railway station with 11 elephants, and a virtual zoo collection, including a giraffe seen here with my friend Terry Darmody N.T. at the Showgrounds.

Years later, I brought the Fossetts Circus Big Top here for an RTE television Show.

They attended the re-opening of the Island Rowing Club.

LEFT: A Pioneer Rally in St. Mary's.

ABOVE: Poet Austin Clark on a visit to
The Nationalist Office.

RIGHT: Senator Des Hanafin marries local girl
Mona Brady at SS. Peter & Paul's Church.

Mick Del brought together some of his former band members for the re-opening of the Collins Hall in 1958.

*Mick Strappe, pictured on right with his brother Jim and their respective wives Terry and Celeste, began his career in journalism with the Munster Tribune and later joined The Nationalist. In the late 50s he wrote The Mick Del Story, so he is the ideal person to recall:*

# The Dancing Years

"All trips down memory lane are exhilarating, but often touched with sadness. As the mind eases into reverse, happy memories of faces and places surface but as the good times are relived, also into focus come thoughts of friends that are no longer with us.

These are recollections of a decade which is laced with nostalgia. It was the era of Mick Del, the Hunt Balls, the dress dances and the ordinary half crown and five bob "hops". Many a romance began while dancing to the bands of the time and many of the relationships formed then have prospered and are still strongly surviving today.

In recalling the dancing scene of the 50's in Clonmel, the past is very much kept alive. Sadly the man, best remembered with affection by the public, revered by dancers and so popular with all - Mick Delahunty is today absent from the bandstand of life. He died unexpectedly, if fittingly, shortly after his band's farewell appearance at The Greenwood Inn, Ardpatrick, Co. Limerick on Saturday, February 29th, 1992. He did not play with the band that night, but at the end of their performance he addressed the crowd. Shortly after stepping off the stage he became ill and died.

Mick Del. had few peers as a danceband leader. His orchestra was recognized as the best in Ireland and he was undoubtedly the biggest celebrity in dancing circles during the 50's. Admired by a huge public throughout the land, he remained unassuming, modest, unspoiled by success and always passionately proud to be a Clonmel man.

The story of Mick Del as a bandleader began on Easter Sunday night 1933 when he led his six piece band onto the stage at The Abbey Hall, Cahir to play for an Old I.R.A Commemoration Dance. It was called "The Harmony Band" and on stage that night with him was the all-Clonmel combo of Mickey Fennessy (violin), his brother Frank (piano), Christy O'Riordan (sax), his brother James (trumpet) and Willie Power (drums). The admission price was 3/- (15p in today's money) including supper. That year Mick Delahunty bought his first new saxophone for £14.00.

Some of the faces associated with Mick Del. bands of the time which always come on-screen during re-runs of these days are Danny McNamara, Mary Mullins, Eddie Roberts (vocalists), Billy Kenrick who also had his own orchestra, Eileen Sloan, Peter Gaffney, Karl Weiss, Paddy Byrne, Billy Murphy, Alex Freiberg, Bennie McNeill who later joined the RTECO, and of course his brothers, Paddy Delahunty who played string bass and Jackie on drums.

One of the most successful dances ever held in the Clonmel Collins Hall was a gala event held on Easter Saturday night, 1958 to mark the occasion of Mick Del's 25th Anniversary as a bandleader. A Mick Delahunty Silver Jubilee Committee headed by Dubliner, J.J. Murphy, Editor of the "Sporting Press", and Mick Del's life long friend, Fethard born, Billy Kenrick as secretary, both now deceased, organised the event and the public who he had always treated with respect fittingly returned the compliment by flocking to the ballroom that night to pay tribute to the Maestro.

Mick Delahunty was a commanding figure in dancehalls across the land but his fame also spread overseas. He won international acclaim when he took his fifteen piece orchestra on English and American tours. He originally went to London in 1951 for the well known Fuller organisation, playing a three week tour in the Irish clubs and returned there in 1957. His orchestra also thrilled packed audiences in Irish clubs in Boston and New York.

*Above right is the Pat McNamara Orchestra line-up, while on right is Enda O'Riordan's Riverside Jazz Band.*

*The montage of dance groups on the opposite page is a selection of those from all over South Tipperary who attended the wide variety of "Dress" dances at the time.*

Other bands high on the popularity list with Clonmel dancers in those days were the Maurice Mulcahy and Jimmy Wiley orchestras from Mitchelstown, The Billy Kenrick Orchestra from Clonmel, The Mick Fogarty Orchestra, Cashel, The Billy Touhy Orchestra from Tipperary Town, The Harry Doherty Band, Carrick-on-Suir, The Riverside Jazz Band, Clonmel, The Sean Healy Band from Carrick-on-Suir, The Twilight Serenaders, Fethard, The Kevin Flynn Orchestra from Cahir, The Pat MacNamara Band from Clonmel, The Denis Cronin Orchestra, Tralee and The Frankie King Orchestra from Waterford.

In addition to the Collins Hall, other very popular Clonmel venues were The Casino in Upper Gladstone Street, The Playfair at Kickham Barracks and the summer stages at The Ball Alley on the Dungarvan Road and The Ragwell and at Goatenbridge near Ardfinnan.

The Hunt Balls and annual dress dances of the time had a glitter, glamour and attraction of their own and some of the big "night's out" were organised by The Clonmel Harrier Hunt, The Kilmoganny Hunt Club, The Scarteen Hunt, The Tipperary Foxhounds and The Waterford Hunt.

Patrons had a wide and varied selection when it came to the annual dress dances and very highly rated amongst these fashionable occasions were The Military Ball at Kickham Barracks, The Island Ball at The Courthouse, The Mental Hospital Ball at St. Luke's Hospital, The Pack of Clubs Ball at the Collins Hall and many others.

ABOVE: *The Committee of the re-opened Casino Ballroom with Canon Barron.*
ABOVE RIGHT: *The Printers Dance Committee for 1956 which includes tenor Frank Patterson, who worked in Slater's Printing Works at that time.*
OPPOSITE PAGE: *At the Mental Hospital Ball.*

Another big occasion and a very special night out in Clonmel was the annual Printer's Dance organised by The Printer's Committee and featuring who else but the one and only Mick Delahunty.
The first indications that it was due was the start of a clever advertising campaign in the local papers T*he Nationalist* and T*he Munster Tribune*. The teaser ads usually began in October and advised you "You've Got Four Hours To Get Out!" . . . on the dance floor and dance your feet off at the Printers Dance.

One of the most successful advertising gimmicks of all was "The Invisible Fish" hoax set up in the front window of Willie Corbett's Printing Works in Parnell Street. A transparent tank was put on display and the public were invited to spot the fish.

It was the talk of the town with some people insisting that they saw a fish in the tank. Others hotly argued that they saw the water moving and there had to be something in there. Of course the organising Printers Devils knew better. But it was original and it worked. The Collins Hall attraction was a sellout.

Dancing in Ardfinnan.

"The Printers" were nights that promised "explosive entertainment" that included free hats, masks, balloons, streamers, (bought from Gings theatrical suppliers, Dublin,) Mr. Moon and of course the song-laden souvenir programmes with the poll-toppers of the day.

*Actor Billy Quinn's stage performance seems to be just too much for Mayor Mick Kilkelly and Mick Delahunty at the Printers' Dance!*

The highlight of the night was the midnight arrival of "Mr. Personality". Some of the most memorable of these over the years were Jimmy O'Dea, Connie Foley of "The Wild Colonial Boy" fame, Patricia Cahill, and later R.T.E's Brendan O'Reilly, boxer Rinty Monaghan, and Tolka Row's Jim Bartley, who now plays "Bella" in Fair City.

These dances were organised by colleagues from the printing houses of Clonmel - The Nationalist, Sporting Press, Slaters and Willie Corbetts. "The Printers" moved out of the Collins Hall twice - once to Cashel and the second time to Fethard.

Also very high on the popularity list was the annual "Mayor's Fund" dance which was organised by the Mayor of the day and also attracted capacity crowds. The money raised was used by the First Citizen to distribute parcels and money vouchers to the needy people of the town.

It was all go and enjoyment at the time and the Clonmel Coursing Club dances were also occasions not to be missed. In February 1959 they advertised a big double attraction - The Clipper Carltons and The Royal Showband. The "Clippers" were on stage in the Collins Hall on Tuesday, February 3rd as a Coursing Carnival attraction (with relief band, The Casino Orchestra) and "The Royal" visit which was described as "The Last Big Dance Before Lent" was listed for February 8th. Dancing on both nights was from 9.00 p.m. to 3.00 a.m. with catering by Jerry Moynihan, Clonmel and the admission was 6/3d (31p today)

Some of the personnel associated with the running of the spacious Collins Hall ballroom which was the mecca for dancers from all over Munster at the time were Willie Fitzgerald (caretaker), Patrick Daly and Patrick O'Connor (door stewards and checkers), Ned Gahan, Paddy Tobin, Johnny Mulcahy, Denis Kane, Willie Hurley, Maurice Flynn (bar staff), Ellen Cashin, May Cashin, Gladys Morley (cloakroom stewards), and the Managers and Directors, Denis Barrett, Paddy Fitzgerald, Enda O'Riordan, Jackie Morrissey, Michael White, Bobby O'Brien and William Morrissey, Architect.

*Below (from left): Jerry Moynihan, Willie Fitzgerald, Ned Gahan and Paddy Fitzgerald.*

Mick Del drove his own car and his brother Paddy drove the bandwagon and regardless of the time they returned to their Clonmel base after every performance. Overnight stop-overs were never involved.

There was exceptional interest in and also vibrant support for traditional Irish dancing and music throughout the area at that time and some memorable sessions were held in Parish Halls, Town Halls and the local dance halls. In the late 1950's, St Patrick's Hall, Clonmel (formerly The Casino) became the Céilí headquarters in Clonmel and regular visitors here were The Knocknagow Ceili Band with vocalist, Sheila Clancy, The Ballinamore Ceili Band and of course The Gallowglass Ceili Band, with vocalists, Patricia Duffy and Jimmy McGarr. Rince was from 8-12 or 9-2 and the luach ranged from 3/6d to 6/3d (37p to 61p).

Just after these times the musical spotlight shifted and the showband circuit started it's roll. Their upbeat music and presentation became addictive for the dancing public. The popularity and appeal of the top bands like "The Royal Showband" from Waterford, fronted by Brendan Bowyer and "The Clipper Carlton" from Strabane featuring Hugo Quinn and many other groups spread like wildfire and the "house full" signs went up wherever they appeared. Rock 'n' Roll and Skiffle Groups also appeared on the scene and who will forget the screaming crowds that poured into the Ritz Cinema for the Clonmel Premiere of Bill Haley's "Rock around the Clock".

The new musical phenomena had arrived, a new era had begun but patrons would never forget the fifties. They were memorable, civilised days, full of enjoyment and fun.

*Rock and Roll time at a teenagers hop.*

Dance Class in the Tech.

An Tostal Beauty Queens with Mayor Taylor.

In the Collins Hall.

The Dominos Showband.

*Aidan Kilkelly was not only a colleague of mine on The Nationalist staff, but a fellow hiker with An Óige. Here he recalls:*

# Happy Days with An Óige

*Freddie plans the route up Carrantuohill, while Redmond Burke appears to be heading home!*

Sometimes referred to as "Mad Carew" by newcomers to An Óige, he was a virtual legend in his own lifetime in mountaineering circles all over Ireland. We knew him as Freddie Carew. He was an enigmatic figure in his usual attire - Castro-style peaked cap and khaki tunic, as he took off across the hills like the wild mountain goats that pervaded the dark recesses of Coumshingaun. A charismatic character, he was a born leader and a paragon where mountaineering was concerned, who tried to inculcate that perfectionist trait of his into all of us. His hiking gear was the quintessence in what was sensible and practical for the hills.

He was a model from his peaked cap to his hob-nailed boots and he led some of the most exciting hikes in the 50's.

An Óige in Clonmel in the late 40's consisted of a few individuals like Peg Barrett, her sister Mary and Betty Coffey, who had already at that time considerable experience of hill walking in Ireland. In fact it was Peg who first took the initiative in the formation of a group of An Óige in Clonmel in 1948 by contacting a number of us whom she thought might be favourably disposed to the idea. She duly arranged a slide show in Clonmel with executive members from Dublin who extolled the virtues of hiking and hostelling with An Oige.

A few enthusiasts immediately joined and having had our first group hike with Peg leading the way on foot from the Gashouse Bridge to Loch Mór, we were on our way. We were immediately captivated by the Comeraghs . . . its lakes and corries.

And, it wasn't too long before we ventured further afield to the Macgillycuddy Reeks with its majestic Carrantuohill, and eventually to all the other wonderful peaks in the country including Brandon, Errigal and Lugnaquilla. Membership of An Óige, with its fine hostels strategically dotted around the country, gave us that greater access to those lovely places.

With excellent photographers in the group at that time like Freddie Carew and John Rossiter we were able to hold our own slide shows displaying the scenic delights of the Comeraghs and the Kerry mountains to potential members. As a result we had an influx of new members and large crowds were turning up at the Gashouse Bridge on Sunday mornings - hail, rain or shine, for the start of long treks to the Comeraghs. And, how we loved to brew up beside a mountain lake on a heather fire with its delightful pungent aroma and sipping strong smokey tea on which you could trot a mouse!

As the 50's moved on, more and more members were utilising the An Óige hostels. They provided cheap overnight accommodation and were ideal bases for hiking and climbing, as well as meeting

people from other lands. Mountain Lodge with its tree-lined avenue ablaze in Springtime and early Summer with beautiful rhododendron and azalea blossoms, was a popular hostel with Clonmel members who used it frequently to climb Galtymore. And many a Hallowe'en party was held there, as well as that memorable farewell party for Mai Williams, one of the groups most enthusiastic members who was leaving for America at the time. It was always a pleasure meeting the affable warden, Paddy Crotty and later his wife who took over following his death.

Ballydavid Wood hostel was also a firm favourite with Clonmel members who spent many a night there, sometimes setting off the next morning across the Galtees and stopping overnight at Mountain Lodge before trekking back again the following day to Ballydavid to pick up their bikes. There was always a great welcome there too from the warden, Mrs. Alice Dowling who had such a high regard for the Clonmel group.

We remember the occasion when sixteen of us loaded our bikes aboard the train in Clonmel for Arthurstown in Co. Wexford. We had a "stopping order" arranged by Edwin Fitzgerald for Campile where we alighted and cycled the short distance to the hostel. We returned home after a great week-end via the ferry from Ballyhack to Passage East which was very basic indeed in those days compared to what it is today. Edwin had another coup when he succeeded in hiring a train from Clonmel to Cahir and back for our annual dinner-dance in the Galtee Hotel where the "young" Pat Mac provided the music for a night of dancing and good fun.

Everyone loved the long week-ends and the fun on the bus which we usually hired for such occasions. The trip that stands out was the one to Connemara to climb the Twelve Bens staying overnight at Mountshannon and Lettermullen hostels. The "cook" on the occasion was "Count" Twomey, back from Australia who aided and abetted by Micheál Moloney, Micky Walsh, "Fish" Ahearne and Willie Powell, produced a succulent meal of steak and onions fit for a king - whatever about the broth!

Individuals and small groups meanwhile were taking off around Ireland in the 50's, as well as hiking in Britain and the Continent . . . Freddie Carew leading parties in the Lake District . . . Paul Gleeson and Leo Wallace popping over there too.

Tony O'Brien doing a solo run on his bike across Europe, stopping off for a few months in Spain . . . a group of us making a week-end attack on Snowdon . . . Tony O'Keeffe and I returning later for a week of climbing in Snowdonia . . .

getting caught in a rain-storm on top of Snowdon . . . managing to make our way down to a mountain pass where we were picked up by British soldiers on manoeuvres who were in as bad a shape as we were.

I got bitten by the "Continental" bug following my first hostelling experience in 1950 with Edmond Symes and Paddy Stapleton in Bavaria where we attended the Oberammergau Passion Play . . . Peg Barrett and her sister Mary were travelling in Italy . . . Leo Wallace and Brendan Long were also in the same neck of the woods . . . Edwin Fitzgerald, Jimmy McCarthy, Betty Lacey and I went hostelling there in 1954 . . . the highlight for us was the Canonisation of Pius X and an early morning climb in the lower slopes of the Alps.

There followed for me some years trekking around Europe with Edwin Fitzgerald . . . remembering our three weeks in Yugoslavia . . . standing on Princip Bridge in Sarajevo . . . our two-day cruise down the Dalmation coast sleeping on deck as we sailed in and out the islands in the Adriatic . . . stopping off for five glorious days in Dubrovnik . . . our exhilirating climb on another occasion in the Tatra mountains between Poland and Czechoslovakia having earlier been stopped by border guards . . . our camera been taken from us as we attempted to "shoot" Kruschev and Bulganin who were just a few feet in front of us at a small railway station near the Russian border where their train stopped during a whistle-stop tour.

Autumn always saw us all back in Ireland with perhaps a trip to Killarney before our season of serious Winter climbing in the Comeraghs began. There was our memorable climb of Carrauntouhill in September of 1956. It is interesting to recall those involved . . . Freddie Carew, Billy Murphy, Patricia Kilkelly,

Lily Carew, Kitty Ryan, Joan O'Brien, Edwin Fitzgerald, Aidan Kilkelly, Mai Williams, Colette Roche, Con Barry, Kathleen O'Brien, Dick Murray, Tony O'Brien, Jimmy Reddin, Gerry King and Des Mullan.

We were back again in Killarney the following year, 1957, for the official opening of Aghadoe House An Óige hostel. It was a very prestigious event with many dignitaries present. A huge jamboree was organised for the week-end with An Óige members from all over Ireland and some international hostellers taking part. Clonmel had a large contingent there as well as set-dancers Tony O'Keeffe, Sean Flaherty, Ann Fitzgerald and Marie Coffey whose performance was very well received.

As the 50's were drawing to a close Justin Nelson produced an excellent short colour-film of over fifty Clonmel An Óige members in the Comeraghs called "Mountain Magic".

It showed the members starting out from town and later trekking across the hills from Coumshingaun to Crottys Lake. Later Justin, Con Barry, Donie Phelan, Joe Purcell and I spent an exhilirating week-end climbing Ben Nevis in Scotland. See the photo of the five of us in the snow near the summit.

And, we availed of the opportunity to visit Frank Roche, father of members Sheila and Colette. He was a manager at the Loch Lomond Hotel having been previously with Hearns Hotel in Clonmel for many years.

Looking back over the years to some earlier hikes . . . a large party of us getting lost in a fog over Coum Dualla . . . wandering down into the Nire Valley at one o'clock in the morning and having to foot-slog it home . . . remembering, too, that lovely lady, Hanora Harte, near the Nire church who used to mind our bikes whilst we took off into the hills sometimes ignoring her warnings not to go up there in the fog . . . and how she would wait anxiously for our return.

*Sheila Roche, Rena Condon and Eithne Maher.*

As we moved into the 60's An Óige as a group began to disintegrate as some members got married and others went away. But Freddie Carew soldiered on despite a serious operation. We lost touch with him a little as we became preoccupied rearing our families. Then we heard the sad news of his death in the Autumn of '85 which brought nostalgic memories flooding back of wonderful days we all had together. His passing marked the end of and era in Clonmel as far as An Óige was concerned.

And, how can we forget those we hiked with . . . pioneers like Paddy Cronin, Biddy O'Brien and others who were part of that small intrepid band in the early days . . . and those that followed on - names not already mentioned . . . Richie McCarthy, Eileen Whelan, Lily O'Donnell, Redmond Burke, Helen Marshall, Nora and Breda McGrath, Joan Condon, Martha Cleary, Theresa Phelan, Jim Fitzgerald, Ivy Dillon, Sean Ryan, Billy Ryan, Mary and Terry Weston, Phil Walsh, Jimmy O'Donnell, Sheila Shanahan, Rosie McEvilly, Phyllis Brady, Maureen O'Brien, Helen Fitzgerald, Josephine Kempton, Joan Patterson, John Wallace, Maureen, Deirdre and Brendan Thornton, Ann Delehunty, Leo Fitzgerald, Eithne Maher, Rene Condon, Bunny and Winnie Dwyer, Ger King, Nora and Joan Sheehan, Mollie Slatery, Jimmy Eviston, Kathleen Maher, Alix Kilkelly, Ann Ruth, Joan Keating, Eamonn Keating, Bernie English, Billy Butler, Des and Joan Cully, Kitty and Peggy Nugent, Calley and Frances Fitzgerald and junior members . . . Philip Daniels, Michael Cremmings, Junior Hackett, Michael Johnson, Pat Fennessy, Jimmy Smith, Michael Fitzgerald, Kevin Hackett, Johnny Delehunty, Thomas Weston . . .

An Óige has had a profound effect on all of us and was such a beautiful episode in our lives that it has left us with the happiest of memories - even after so many years.

**Des Mullan**, *who is currently* Political Correspondent *of the* Evening Herald, *arrived in Clonmel just a few months before I did. Here he recalls:*

# The Summer of '55

"It was a great Summer. The weather was so good Bulmers were working around the clock to keep the country supplied with those sparkling flagons of cider. The fly hatches swarmed on the gently flowing Suir - not to mind the Anner, Tar, Nire and a hundred trout filled streams from Slievenamon to the Comeraghs.

Mick Delahunty and his Big Band were heading on the Seaside Express for another Summer season in Youghal's Showboat, with crowds of his admiring followers from the South Tipperary capital already there before him. And most important of all, down off the Davis Road the greyhounds were running. For a young man immersed in the lore and legend of the greyhound, Clonmel and a job there, was Heaven in that mid-year of 1955.

Along the approaches to the town and in the streets telegraph poles and dead walls bore blue and white teaser posters heralding a momentous coming event. There was no mystery about it really - everyone knew it was the launch of the *Munster Tribune*. Editor Fintan Faulkner and the seven local business and professional people backing it were about to take on the century old *Nationalist* steeped in the tradition and history of Tipperary. The brash newcomer with its page one headlines and pictures

exploded on the scene like a starburst, and started a circulation war that was to change journalism in the town forever.

*The Nationalist* met the new challenge head-on. It matched every move *The Tribune* made. When the new arrival put a new van on the road with the title emblazoned all over it, *The Nationalist* got a bigger one. When *The Tribune* hired a staff photographer, *The Nationalist* hired Justin Nelson - and Clonmel has never regretted that particular piece of good fortune! Every facet of news and sports reporting took on a new urgency in South Tipperary and the bordering counties which were the circulation areas of both papers. Local councillors found they had new outlets for their policies, and urban, city and county councils suddenly were getting acres of publicity as both papers vied for the news.

Barney Cavanagh, a young Dungannon man headed the reporting team after the short journey from the *Kilkenny People*. He took the writing of a Town Talk column, while I was assigned the Inquisitive Reporter Page, a job that brought me to every town and village in County Tipperary and quite a few in the bordering counties of Waterford Cork, Kilkenny and Limerick. We were later joined by Mick Strappe straight out of the Christian Brothers and Michael Hogan who took over the GAA pages. Michael was to die tragically young after joining the *Irish Press*.

It was a big journalistic coup for editor Fintan Faulkner when he induced the legendary Dan Breen T.D. to write a weekly column for *The Tribune* . . . *"From the Desk of Dan Breen"*. Dan didn't stay too long at his desk! He stuck it for a few months. Writing columns did not come easy to him and they were mostly of the homespun philosophy variety. One I can remember at election time was urging people to get out and vote. "Exercising the franchise" as he put it, was a privilege dearly won.

I think it was Brendan Long who first told me the story of Dan's election campaigns. It was said that all he had to do to get elected was "rattle the bullets". This was a reference to his still carrying bullet fragments in his legs after his many battles in the War of Independence. There were even those who went so far as to claim that when he coughed, the bullets still in his lungs also rattled!

Anyway, Dan Breen (pictured above at Kilfeacle) in a towering rage was a sight to behold. The normally placid old warrior seldom lost his temper, but when he did his fury knew no bounds. There was the night in Hearns Hotel - the occasion a farewell dinner for Fintan Faulkner who was leaving to take up an editorial position with the Irish Press. Dan was a special guest and had just arrived from the Mount Melleray Monastry where he had finished a retreat. It was soon after a major political battle for the headquarters of the newly formed Bord na gCon. Dan and his political colleagues had fought what they thought was the winning fight. He departed to New York secure in the knowledge that Clonmel was to be the headquarters having beaten off Limerick. I witnessed his rage as he told the story. "I came back from the States to find they had given it to Limerick - a town noted only for two things - its whores and its Confraternity" he stormed!

It was ironic that only a short time after Dan's diatribe against the awarding of the Bord na gCon headquarters to Limerick that the first Chairman of the Bord, Dr. Paddy Maguire, should address a gathering in the very same room, and announce a major policy programme for the Bord. That was the more serious side of the greyhound industry in Clonmel.

There was a different side - ranging from the historical headquarters of the Irish Coursing Club on Davis Rd, the printing of the greyhound newspaper "The Sporting Press", previously the Coursing Calendar, and the greyhound men - and women too! Especially the women, of whom Miss Kitty Butler, Sec. of the I.C.C. was the greatest. Or as Mayor Jim Taylor once described her in the immortal words - "The Queen of Greyhounds"! That was on the famous occasion of the civic reception for that great coursing trainer Dick Ryan who trained the Waterloo Cup winner "Old Kentucky Minstrel" in the '56/'57 coursing season.

All the coursing "Greats" celebrate in style at the Pack O' Clubs Ball.

On left is "Fly" Kennedy.

Clonmel abounded in greyhound characters, but straight out of the pages of Damon Runyon must have come "Fly" Kennedy and "Caution" Fitzgerald. Professional gamblers and greyhound owners, their partnership struck terror into the Dublin bookmakers when they raided Shelbourne Park or Harold's Cross with their latest "flyer". Not far behind them in bringing off "jobs" either at the local track or in Dublin were the brothers Chris and Eamon McGrath and Tony Harney.

The National Coursing meeting at Powerstown Park was the great greyhound event of the year for Clonmel, but for the true coursing men locally the Clonmel and District Coursing club was the centre of things. Throughout the season they ran the Sunday open coursing meetings of which the Brassey Cup was the highlight.

Commander Brassey hosted the celebration of the final at his imposing mansion just outside the town. If a little bitch owned by Jimmy Morrissey from Carrick-on-Suir hadn't crashed into a telegraph pole in the centre of the coursing field a dog called "Two Tribunes" could have won the course and gone on to win the final, and I would have collected the Brassey Cup.

*On right, Commander Brassey presents his trophy following the final of the Open Coursing competition, while below is the organising Committee of the National Coursing meeting at Powerstown Park.*

Sunday morning in the Spring of 1956 with a full turn out of open coursing enthusiasts at Ballingarane, below and right.

The greyhound men met in either Michael Phelan's "The Solid Man" in O'Connell St. or in Annie Kehoe's at the lower end of Parnell St. Over large bottles or flagons of cider - or even both!, the day's coursing was analysed. And after the races at the track the winners celebrated and divided the spoils. Annie Kehoe presided over the establishment famous for the diversity of its clientele. "County"folk mixed with mountainy men from the hill farms of the Comeraghs. Annie was an avid reader of all things Royal. She could be immersed in the *Town and Country* magazine or any publication for the "County set". When Waterford Crystal made its big comeback about then she had her shelves sparkling with goblets, tumblers and brandy bowls. The horsey set or anyone she deemed worthy of it were served their spirits in Waterford glasses, the "large bottle" brigade had to make do with the plain stout glass!

"The Solid Man" pub was privy to many a "greyhound job" plotted in the snugs at the rear of this old fashioned pub. Only afterwards did you hear of the coup. Johnny Morrissey, foreman in the Sporting Press printing establishment was one of the shrewdest greyhound men in Clonmel. He only kept a few dogs at a time but they were always top class. It was no bother to him to bring off a job in Shelbourne Park and with a cross channel buyer alerted to see his charge win - pocket a £1,000 or more afterwards for the sale.

Johnny was a fine angler too. One morning early while exercising his greyhounds along the Suir above Irishtown he spotted a salmon in a pool. He had to go to work but at lunchtime he hurried home, got his rod, caught the salmon,and still returned to work within his lunch hour. You could do that sort of thing in Clonmel in those days.

About that time I heard of the "Hermit of Lackendarra". He was a hermit wandering the Comeragh mountains. Women hikers in the mountains had been frightened by him, it was said. They need not have feared because poor old Lackendarra Jim literally lived under a huge rock on the Waterford side of the mountains just below the lovely lake of Counshingaun. Tommy Carey, T*he Tribune* photographer and myself found him there after a few unsuccessful attempts to locate him earlier.

He was a shy lonely man, said to have been shellshocked in the First World War. He only ventured out of the mountains to collect his pension in Rathgormack. Far from frightening anybody, he scuttled for shelter at the approach of strangers. Paddy Melody of Ballymacarbry had told us that "Lack" (as he was known locally) was partial to a drop of whiskey. A wisp of smoke over a rock finally showed us he was "at home". He emerged eventually to our call, his smoke blackened face grimy and creased. His bushy beard under a slouch hat equally blackened with the smoke from his fire under the rock. But "Lack" while courteous and thankful for the few jars had little to say. He got his name from a ridge called Lackendarra, which stretches from Counshingaun to Crotty's Lake in the Comeraghs.

We left him to the solitude and his rock haven in the mountains. The next we heard of him was when he was taken to Dungarvan Hospital seriously ill. Against all his protests they cut off his beard - for hygienic reasons, it was said. He subsequently made world headlines through *Irish Press* reporter John Scarry's double page spread in *Wide World* magazine and news stories put out by the old Irish News Agency written by the late John Healy.

Many a happy day was spent in those same mountains with members of Clonmel's An Óige. Freddie Carew was one of the leading lights, as you can read in Aidan Kilkelly's piece in this book. One Summer he invited a young Nigerian, studying nursing in Coventry for a holiday in Clonmel. Michael Obiefuna joined our group for a hike to Coumfea above the Nire Valley. He told me his story, and the following weekend *The Tribune* carried it with the heading,"The Man from Nimo-Awka".

The truth is stranger than fiction or the long arm of coincidence bit comes nearly twelve years later. When we bade goodbye in Clonmel, Michael Obiefuna disappeared out of our lives - for good as we thought. On a second trip for Independent Newspapers to war-torn and famine-stricken Biafra, I was travelling with a Dublin Holy Ghost priest Fr. Tim Nolan in the northern sector of the dwindling Biafran territory. Bored with the endless miles of brown bush countryside and for want of something to say I asked Fr. Tim where we were at that point. "We're coming to a village called Nimo" he said. After a little reflection I said, " I once heard of a village of that name, but it was called Nimo-Awka" .

"Ah yes", he said, "Nimo is the village and Awka is the province". I told him the man concerned was named Michael Obienfuna, who was once a male nurse in Coventry. The surname, he said, is like Murphy in Ireland - thousands of them. We drove on a few miles when Fr. Tim suddenly said, "Hold on a minute, I think there is a nurse in the clinic in Nimo of that name".

But we were bypassing Nimo heading for the frontline near Onitcha where Fr. Tim's shell wrecked church lay abandoned. He promised to call to Nimo on the way back. It was dark when we finally stopped at Nimo, Fr. Tim said he would go and have a look at the clinic to see if Michael was there, and if he could possibly be the same person who was in Clonmel all those years before.

After a 15 minute wait he emerged from the clinic with a bearded Nigerian - but there was no mistaking the smiling eyes of Michael Obiefuna! We were both stunned, and he said, " Des, to think I should have to greet you like this in my country, unable to offer any hospitality". His clinic was surrounded by crowds of starving Biafran families. We chatted for a while and left him a parting gift of what tinned food we could spare. Later we sent him over a food parcel on the Concern ship "Columba".

*The Evening Herald* carried the story and photo of our shaking hands in the best Livingstone-Stanley tradition - . . . "Mr. Mullan, I presume."

RIGHT: *No, it's not a jaunt around the lakes of Killarney, but the occasion was a ladies walking race from Clonmel, when spectators used a variety of transports to travel out the Kilsheelan Road, and so watch the race develop.*

The girls on the left were members of the Island Boat Club, who were no doubt keeping an eye on the athletic young men (right) who formed winning teams in the various rowing regattas.

ABOVE: With no swimming pool, the river Suir was the only place to be when temperatures got hot.

They gathered in the Sportsfield on the Western Road.

Confirmation Day 1960 at SS. Peter & Paul's.

*St. Patrick's Well on the National Feast Day.*

Traffic came to a standstill in Cahir as crowds knelt in the town Square for the Corpus Christi Procession.

TOP LEFT and LEFT: The members of the Red Cross and Knights of Malta came together for a social function in the Collins Hall.

ABOVE: The Lane Band is pictured at the Sportsfield on the Western Road.

TOP RIGHT: The forerunners of Riverdance.

BOTTOM RIGHT: Boys from the High School visit Kickham Barracks.

Note the absence of the Tech., and the Ford
Prefects and Austin 30s which line the street
in another familiar flooding scene.

Dr. O'Connell with the teaching staff of Clonmel Tech.

LEFT: As I mentioned earlier, Travel Agent Pat Rafferty helped in no small way to have me assigned by Aer Lingus to be part of the airline's inaugural jet flight from Shannon to New York. Here Pat (on the right of the picture) is seeing off a group of pilgrims bound for Lourdes from the railway station.

RAFFERTY TRAVEL AGENCY

LEFT: Flooding has been a problem in the Suir Valley for generations. The group on left gathered in an effort to solve the Anner floods. It includes quite a collection of local politicians, including Mick Davern, Frank Loughman, Jackie Ahessy, John Kennedy and Jimmy Murphy.

RIGHT: A Skittles team from the Prior Park area.

LEFT: *Peggy Maher (centre front row) was a keen sportswoman, and was Ladies Captain in 1958 when she presented her prizes in the Summer sunshine at the Golf Club.*

BELOW: *This was one of the first groups I photographed in 1955, and it features local British Army ex-servicemen at a commemoration ceremony in Clonmel.*

All twelve members of the Marshall family from Ballypatrick were setting off for a day at the seaside when I took their picture.

"The Lily of Killarney" with Frank Patterson (left), Michael Burke from Cashel (centre) with Mary Britton, who is still very much involved in staging musicals, looking over his shoulder.

Having gone to the same school as the great tenor John McCormack, I have had a particular interest in the singing career of Clonmel's **Frank Patterson**, who has carved out quite a successful career since going to live in New York. In recent years I have featured Frank in a special hour long programme recorded at the Trump Taj Mahal in Atlantic City, as well as inviting him to co-host a very successfull season of Summer Cabaret with Bibi on RTE television.
Here he recalls:

# Voices on my Mind

"Funny things can happen while you are in your hotel room! On tour recently, after a concert in Palm Beach, Florida, I was flicking through the channels on the television, when my attention was caught by the strains of "When Other Lips" from the Bohemian Girl. The stars of the show were Laural & Hardy - in acting roles of course and in hilarious form. All the old tunes were there, bringing back memories of Clonmel, old friends and wonderful voices.

Sitting there with the Floridian sun streaming through the windows, I was back hearing the tenor voice of Tom Hogan, who with soprano, Nellie Corbett starred in many of the operas in Magner's Theatre under the baton of Professor James A. White. It all came flooding back - the deep sepulchral tones of Paddy Dockery from Templemore and the refined elegance of Paddy Hickey's baritone. In those days, the town was bursting with vocal talent, much of it coached by Billy O'Brien, the organist in

ABOVE: *The boys choir in SS. Peter & Paul's Church, with young Frank Patterson, fourth from left in the back row. I have to thank John Shea (third from right front row) for letting me have this photograph.*

RIGHT: *Alice McCormack and Phil Burns in "The Lily of Killarney".*

97

the Friary. Names that come to mind were Sheila Cairns, John Roche (who later sang in Covent Garden), Michael Burke of Cashel, Biddy King, Phil Burns, Monica Cullen, Michael Vaughan and Larry Bates, not to mention my colleagues in the tenor line of St. Mary's Choral Society! We certainly made sure we were heard.

Both my parents, Seamus and Mae were lifelong members of the Society, so it was no small wonder that I was introduced to the stage at a very young age. I made my debut as a Page in the *Gondeliers*, while a young Andy O'Mahoney, who is now one of the best known voices on RTE radio, was the Drummer Boy in that production.

By 1955 and the production of the *Bohemian Girl* I had joined my father in the "Gentlemen of the Chorus" and likewise for *Martha* in '56. By '57 I had left the chorus, when producer Brendan Long gave me the role of "Christophe" in the *Bells of Corneville*.

The Society's next production was *The Lily of Killarney* which we took to the Festival of Kerry. This photograph shows part of our group departing from Clonmel railway station accompanied by the Mayor Michael Kilkelly. I'm in the picture myself too.

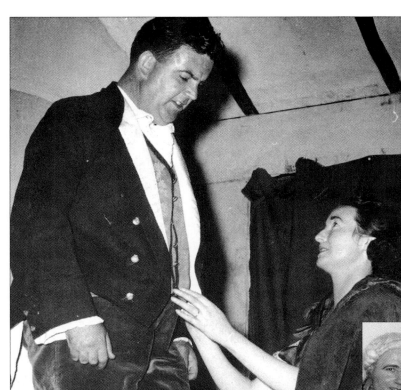

ABOVE: *Nellie Corbett as the "Colleen Bawn" with Tom Hogan.*

RIGHT: *Some of the ladies and gentlemen of the chorus.*

Among those taking part in the *Lily of Killarney*, I recall Nellie Corbett, Phil Burns, Alice McCormack, Nancy Browne, Tom Hogan, Michael Burke, Jack Griffin, Paddy Dochrey, Dan Hogan, Paddy Hickey, Jim Boles, Andy Phelan, Mary Britton and Eddie Owens. As usual the conductor was Professor James White. Next came *Maritana* in 1959, in which I played the Captain of the Guard with Phil Burns in the title role.

I can still see Tom Morrissey, Andy Phelan and Paddy Condon (whose other love was tennis), stretching for those high notes with my father Seamus and myself aiding and abetting them! How those sopranos, altos and basses envied us! They were led by such stalwarts as Nancy Owens, Mickey Farrell and Jack Griffin, with the by-play directed by Tommy Meagher. I remember too the dedication of people like Simon Denny who helped make the sets, and enthusiastic members like Esther Mulcahy and the late Dolly Butler.

Brendan Long brought us to a new level, elevating me to the rank of principal. "Barney Wattletoes" in *Knocknagow* was to be my vehicle to stardom, but the emigrant train took me away to Dublin, and Jim O'Shea grabbed the moment , but in 1964, I was invited back as one of the soloists for the *"Gilbert and Sullivan Fantasia"* in the Regal Theatre.

*The Choral Society members under their conductor Professor James White also contributed to the many religious occasions – like (on right) coming out of SS. Peter & Paul's to start the Corpus Christi Procession through the streets. All of the familiar faces are there, such as Tom Hogan, Paddy Condon, Jim O'Shea, Joe Byrne, Paddy Hickey, Simon Denny, Tom Kavanagh, etc.*

Hillview Tennis Club was another great place to hear voices! The aforementioned Paddy Condon's cry of "Oh! No!" (when his ball hit the net) was of operatic proportions. His battles with Don Binchy of the South Tipp Tennis Club, were legendary. One would have needed a High Court Judge to umpire! As those were the days of grass courts, on the way up the lane, you would only hear the sound of tennis balls against cat-gut without that dreadful squeak of sneakers that you hear nowadays. On summer evenings we played men's and mixed doubles. Good lady players were in abundance with stars like Bridie Byrne, Joan Dougan, Annie Heffernan, Pat Long, Sheila Maher, and many more.

*Winners all at Hillview -*

BELOW: *The tennis champions with Ernie Hogan and Bill Crowley.*

RIGHT: I *notice the ladies Pitch and Putt winners have nine trophies between the eight of them. Perhaps one member is missing from the photo!*

This Hillview Club tennis group contains most of the players whom Frank has mentioned in his article, although he himself was obviously missing on this occasion. However, he is included in the picture below, which features his other sporting activity - table tennis.

The men, always in shining white, seemed to live in the place. Looking out on the courts, you could count on seeing or hearing Don Keating, Ernie Hogan, Sean Redmond, (another tenor), and when Kevin Pyke had no challengers on the table tennis circuit, he brought his skills onto grass. I can still hear his infectious laugh when he made a passing shot. He was a product of "Hillview in Winter" when table tennis ruled and everybody's goal was to beat Kevin. We all tried! The challengers came one by one; Enda Riordan, Mickey Walsh, Niall O'Neill, even yours truly and we all came to the same fate . . . defeat - usually in straight sets and always to the sound of Kevin's gleeful laughter.

Yes Clonmel to me was truly a town of voices. Walking around the town you would always hear; "Hello there", "A soft auld day, isn't it?", "Miserable weather - although it might brighten up later" Everybody expressed themselves in their own inimitable way. In the morning returning from early Mass, Brother Moloney always had a cheery word. Later as I'd stroll whistling down the Back Passage to work in Slater Bros. on Davis Rd., Frank Burns would greet Duke (my dog) and myself with "Good morning to both of you". From the Redemptorist in the pulpit during Mission week to Fr. Cyril O.F.M. in the Friary declaiming to the back of the Friary that the golfers were to stay to the end of Mass, it was one endless stream of vocal diversity.

The voice that's mostly on my mind, and the sweetest voice of all was the soprano in our kitchen in Ard na Greine. My mother, Mae sang like a lark from early morning as she went from one chore to another. My sister Imelda, brothers Maurice and Noel and I were constantly reminded in song, to "Count Your Blessings, One by One".

*Bridie Condon (centre back row) was an excellent tennis player.*
*Barney Cavanagh (page 140) mentions Bridie and husband Joe, who provided him with homely accommodation in Irishtown.*

Even before I came to Clonmel I had heard local tenor Tom Hogan perform on Radio Éireann on many occasions. Tom was happy to appear in any singing role with either St. Mary's or SS. Peter & Paul's Choral Society. On the occasion these pictures were taken he had a leading role in "The Desert Song". (See newspaper advert. on page 106), together with Sheila Cairns who was also a local favourite.

ABOVE: *The chorus line in the SS. Peter & Paul's Choral Society's Minstrel Show at the Regal.*

LEFT: *Celebration time with the members of the SS. Peter & Paul's Dramatic Society annual social, which was attended by the Mayor Michael Kilkelly.*

BELOW: *The newspaper cutting announcing the Society's up-coming production. The admission prices, with the best seats costing less than 20p, make interesting reading compared with to-day's theatre prices.*

RIGHT: *Some of the ladies who took part, together with "The Red Shadow" himself, Larry Bates.*

SS. Peter & Paul's Choral Society
— Proudly presents —

# The Desert Song

(By arrangement with Samuel French, Ltd.)

AT THE

## CLONMEL THEATRE

ON

WEDNESDAY, THURSDAY, FRIDAY, SATURDAY, SUNDAY

### Sept. 25, 26, 27, 28 and 29

*

Book and Lyrics by Otto Harbach. Oscar Hammerstein 2 and Mandel. Music by Sigmund Romberg.

**DOORS OPEN 7.45          OVERTURE 8.30**
**ADMISSION 3 / 6 , 2 / 6, 2 / - and 1 / 6**

Booking at Devlin's Gladstone Street, Clonmel . commencing MONDAY 16th. inst. BOOKING HOURS 10 a.m. to 12.30 p.m. and 3 p.m. to 6 p.m. (Closed Half-day Thursday) Telephone 330.

# Clonmel Group Stage Colourful Opera

ALL the exciting glamour and romance of the East is brought to the stage by the SS. Peter and Paul's Choral and Dramatic Society, in Sigmund Romberg's musical play "The Desert Song," which will run at the Municipal Theatre, Clonmel, from the 25th to the 29th of September.

Mr. Larry Bates, in the principal male lead, "The Red Shadow," is the owner of a very fine barytone voice which came into prominence at the Society's Minstrel Shows. Since then he has been very much

Sheila Cairns, a busy housewife with three children—will be heard to full advantage in the role of Margo Bonvalet, who plays opposite the General's son Pierre, alias "The Red Shadow." When the Society first

*Parnell Street with the Ritz Cinema (on right) mentioned in the following pages.*

*Edmond Symes was one of the friendly faces in the newspaper staff who made me most welcome when I first joined in 1955.*
*He was soon to take up the important post of Editor of Dáil debates in Leinster House. Here he writes about:*

# Clonmel's Cinemas and Theatres

My memories of Clonmel in the fifties are coloured by that phenomenon which was then the favourite pastime of millions all over the world, going to the pictures or "the flicks", the last no doubt derived from the flickering images which enthralled, and even terrified, our grandparents around the turn of the century.

In the decade before the widespread appearance of television here, the movies provided a welcome escape from the hardships of the not too affluent post war years. In Clonmel everybody eagerly looked forward to the forthcoming films. Normally, the programme changed twice or three times a week, so patrons could see a different film each night.

Of course I was in a privileged position, envied by my friends, since I had free entry to both cinemas, the Oisin and the Ritz, due to my father being manager of the Oisin, and earlier of the Clonmel Theatre. (By the 1950s I had an additional claim for a free ticket since I now wrote the film column for the *Nationalist*.) My father, W.B.Symes, was brought to Clonmel by T.A. Morris, who had built the Oisin Theatre in 1921. In the thirties, both the Oisin Theatre and the former Magners (now the Regal) were bought by William O'Keeffe of Prior Park, who formerly had a drapery business in O'Connell St.

# THE CLONMEL THEATRE

Telephone Clonmel 52   --(MAGNER'S)-- Manager J.G. PFOUNDS

### Look Out for RE-OPENING of above Theatre on
### EASTER MONDAY, March 28th. 1921 Matinee at 3

#### WITH ALL-STAR PROGRAMME FOR THE WEEK

**THERE WILL BE A COMPLETE CHANGE OF PROGRAMME THREE TIMES WEEKLY MONDAY, WEDNESDAY and FRIDAY.**

This Theatre De Luxe is the finest, Healtiest and Largest Provincial Theatre in Ireland; it has all the very latest and most modern equipment in every detail - heating, ventilation, seating etc. Two of the very best and latest pattern Projectors are installed for the projection of the pictures, which will give absolutely rock-steady and flickerless pictures. The largest pictures in Ireland will be shown. Nothing but the very best and latest released pictures, passed by the Dublin Censors, will be screened, and dramatic, Variety and Operatic Companies will be booked when available.

**The Orchestral arrangements are well looked after, and the very latest Popular Selections will be rendered.**

Nothing has been left undone to cater for public comfort and amusement, and the Management will spare no efforts to do everything possible to please the public.

### The Prices of Admission will be the People's Popular Prices.

There will be two matinees every week at 3 O'clock.

Watch this space for further announcements re time of opening and particulars of programme.

#### EVERYTHING USED IN THE CONSTRUCTION OF THIS THEATRE IS OF IRISH MANUFACTURE AND BUILT BY IRISH LABOUR IN IRELAND

*This quaint advertisement appeared in* The Nationalist *in 1921 to announce the re-opening of Magner's Theatre on Davis Road. It was re-opened again in 1956 by the then Minister for Defence, Gen. Sean McKeown, who was welcomed by the Mayor Denis E. Burke, who also gave a civic reception to Hilton Edwards and Michael MacLiammoir pictured in the Council Chamber with Town Clerk, J.V. Nolan.*

During the thirties the Oisin was used for theatrical performances, while the Clonmel Theatre, as Magners was now known, was the only cinema. Athough my father had grown up with the cinema business, he was also very much at home with the various theatrical people who appeared at the Oisin. These included the theatrical companies of Lord and Lady Longford, Edwards/ MacLiammor, and Anew McMaster. The latter was a particular friend of his, and instrumental in arranging my one and only stage appearance - as a page in Macbeth, when I was about 10 years old.

My father was also popular with the many variety artistes who regularly performed on the stage of the Oisin. These included Jimmy O'Dea, Noel Purcell and Frank O'Donovan. I have very pleasant memories of Frank - a real trouper. His hit song, which would always "pull the house down " in Clonmel, was "Sitting on the Bridge below the Town", but he also wrote "On the One Road", which later became a favourite marching song of the FCA. He became an even bigger star in the TV era, appearing as Battie Brennan in the popular RTE series, "The Riordans".

The outbreak of the second World War in 1939, when one would have expected entrenchment, saw instead an expansion of the cinema business in the town. The Oisin was completetely modernised and re-opened in September 1939, just a fortnight after the war began, as "Clonmel's Intimate Cinema". There were to be two programmes each week, but the opening film was so important that it would run for an entire week. It was the film version of George Bernard Shaw's "*Pygmalion*", with Leslie Howard and Wendy Hiller. The programme also included a travelogue and a Walt Disney "*Silly Symphony*". Other movies to appear shortly afterwards included "*The Great Waltz*", "*The Citadel*", "*The Mikado*" and "*Goodbye Mr. Chips*".

Just six months later, on Saturday, 23rd. March 1940, a brand new modern cinema opened in Parnell Street - the Ritz. Unlike the other theatres, it was built primarily as a cinema and proved very popular. It opened with "*Stanley and Livingstone*" starring Spencer Treacy and Sir Cedric Hardwicke, and I was privileged to attend and enjoy that first night. It is interesting to recall the admission charges of a shilling and 8 pence for a seat in the balcony, the back balcony was 1/4d, and admission to "the pit" was just 4d or about 2p nowadays. So now Clonmel had no fewer than three cinemas.

However by the 50s the number had reverted to just two. The Clonmel Theatre no longer operated as a cinema and the position obtaining in the 30s was now reversed, films being shown in the Oisin, with theatrical performances, concerts,and even boxing matches being held in the Clonmel Theatre (The Regal).

*Cork actor James N. Healy as he appeared in John B. Keane's "Sive"*
*in the Regal Theatre.*

*Mayor Sean Treacy received actor Cyril Cusack in the Town Hall where, with J. V. Nolan, they inspected the historic Mayoral chain.*

member of the Franciscan community and performed by the Abbey Players - among whom was my friend and colleague on *The Nationalist*, Brendan Long.

During this period also the Regal was up for sale, and the Clonmel Corporation was debating its purchase. By 1951 the deal was done, and Clonmel was probably unique among provincial towns in having its own municipal theatre. Lord Longford, speaking from the stage at the end of his first visit to the theatre under its new owners, praised the enterprise of the civic fathers, and declared, "I know of no city or town in Ireland which has so fine a theatre in the ownership of its own people". For an admission price of just three shillings (15p) one had the best seat in the house for such productions

In 1950 the town was celebrating the tercentenary of the famous siege of Clonmel, and a highlight of the commemorative programme was a performance in the Regal of a play written by Fr. Cyril O'Mahony, a

as Anew McMaster's "*The Importance of Being Earnest*", "*King Lear*" "*Julius Caesar*" and the ever popular "*Merchant of Venice*". I don't think we realised at the time what wonderful theatrical fare was so easily, and relatively cheaply, available to us. The dance was not forgotten either, with regular visits from the Cork Ballet Group under Joan Denise Moriarty.

Great use was made of the Theatre by the two Clonmel Choral Societies, St. Mary's under James White and SS Peter and Paul's under Xavier Gibson. There were frequent concerts. A favourite singer of the time was Frank Ryan, the Co. Waterford tenor. Locals to appear with him included soprano Sheila Morrissy, comedian Willie Corbett, and the one and only Mick Del.

Radio Éireann was supporting the arts even in those days. The then Radio Éireann Light Orchestra, under Dermot O'Hara, accompanied the St. Mary's Choral Society at one of their concerts. But Clonmel could provide its own instrumentalists also. Another concert featured the Clonmel Light Orchestra under Xavier Gibson and included impersonations of Al Jolsen by P.J. Powell.

I think it was in the early fifties that Clonmel had what was up to then the nearest thing to a film premiere, with all of the razzmatazz of personal appearances by the stars. On this occasion there was only one star, but she was a very special one, as she came from the town. Joan Kenny, formerly of Prior Park, starred in the Rank film, *"Talk of a Million"* along with Jack Warner and Barbara Mullen. She had been living in London where she made her name as a photographic model. *"Talk of a Million"* was, as far as I know, her first film. At the premiere in Clonmel, my father went to town on the publicity, and really made it an occasion. He received Joan with her friends and presented her with a bouquet of white tulips. Needless to say, the cinema was thronged.

It was a memorable night for all, particularly myself, because I had known Joan through her brother, the late Phil Kenny, who had been a school pal of mine. As the film columnist of *The Nationalist*, I was deputed to interview the young star whom I hadn't seen for years. Despite her success, she was a most pleasant, friendly young lady, and a pleasure to interview.

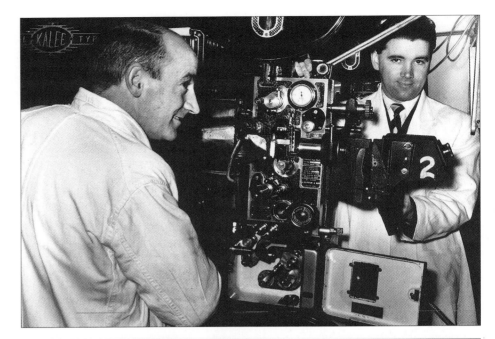

TOP: *The film projectionists at the Ritz.*

ABOVE: *Members of Samuel Beckett's "Waiting for Godot" who performed in the Regal Theatre following their six months run at the Pike Theatre in Dublin.*

112

The start of the 60s saw a cloud on the cinematic horizon - television was on its conquering way. In the early hours of Sunday, 17th December 1966, ironically when a film called "A *Patch of Blue*" had been shown the previous night, the Oisin was burned to the ground with only the familiar facade remaining. The fire was detected at 3 a.m. by Sgt. J. Davis who alerted the fire brigade, but the cinema was doomed despite the best efforts of Clonmel Brigade assisted by brigades from Carrick and Cahir. Fortunately they managed to save the adjoining premises, O'Gorman's Drapery and the Exhibition House. Film buffs may be interested to know that "A *Patch of Blue*" (still in its metal container) was salvaged from the wreckage of the projection room. It starred Sidney Potier and Shelly Winters.

Clonmel then had only one cinema, the Ritz, and the position remained so until 1968, when the Corporation leased the Regal to a Dublin Company to run as a cinema, with the proviso that it be available for theatrical and concert performances also. On Sunday 22nd December of that year, the first film was shown on an impressive wide screen. It was "*The Good, the Bad and the Ugly*" starring Clint Eastwood. A well known Clonmel man, Paddy Condon, was the new manager.

Following the showing of "*The Big Country*" starring Gregory Peck and Burl Ives, the Ritz finally closed its doors on 18th Sept. 1976. I had seen it being built. In its place, stands the fine new building for the Clonmel Credit Union. The Oisin and the Ritz are gone, but the Regal is a survivor. In 1988 it was turned into a three screen cinema, but it too closed its doors in 1995. Not for long though, for I was pleased to read that it has been bought by a Clonmel couple, Larry and Helen O'Keeffe, who have completely renovated it and provided the town with an excellent 850 seat modern theatre. It was officially opened on 2nd November '95 and indeed I wish it long life and every success.

ABOVE: *They helped renovate the Regal Theatre.*

RIGHT: *Mr. W. B. Symes.*

My father retired at the start of the 60s when television was closing down cinemas all over the world, but even then he was not pessimistic. "There will always be young people who will want to go out for their entertainment", he used say. When to-day I see the crowds flocking to the multiplex cinemas in our cities and towns including now, Clonmel, I often think of him and reflect on how right he was.

Items of farming interest were always given comprehensive coverage in The Nationalist.

The group on left were the shareholders of the Suir Island Dairy which opened in 1956, while the groups below were from the Clonmel and Lisronagh branches of Macra na Feirme.

OPPOSITE PAGE: Farmers from the Bansha area setting off on an outing.

When the Irish troops were sent to the Congo, there was a huge march past ceremony in Dublin's O'Connell Street. I was there to capture the historic departure of these – the first to serve overseas, many of whom were stationed in Kickham Barracks.

Time for a rest following the climb to the Holy Year Cross in the Comeragh foothills.

Sean Treacy was Mayor when Canon Walsh from St. Mary's blessed the site for the new Árd Fatima houses.

**Brendan Long** *became Editor of* The Nationalist *after I had left the paper, on the death of W.C. Darmody. Here he recalls his*

# Memories of Tommy O'Brien

"He was one of those people who caused one, however unconsciously, to fall into the trap of considering him eternal. Indeed if it occurred to one to surmise what age he was, the characteristic bounce with which he carried himself, the stentorian energy of his salutation, and a visage which somehow suggested he was more beardless than shaven, remarkably unlined, a sort of baby face, would inevitably frustrate the exercise. He couldn't possibly be as young as his boyish appearance and the ebullience of his manner insisted.

What turned out to have been the very last time I spoke to my former editor and friend, Tommy O'Brien, was in a Clonmel supermart. We came face to face coming from opposite ends of an aisle of groceries. He addressed me - (as was his wont with everybody), as if I were a public meeting. He wanted to know what records, if any, I had brought back from a recent visit to Germany. I noticed for the first time, and with a pang, that he was suddenly aged. Not long after that last encounter there was the sad news of his passing. One of RTE's greatest assets, a sort of national institution, had gone to his eternal reward.

It was under Tommy's editorship that in the mid-forties I had embarked at the age of seventeen on a career in journalism. Having already at that stage developed a taste for what is loosely termed "Classical Music", it was perhaps inevitable that as well as supervising my training in the craft of newspapering, he was also impelled to introduce me to the delights of his vast gramophone record library. His patent enthusiasm at sharing it with those receptive of his guidance led him to advance along astute lines my musical as well as my journalistic education.

I was indeed an early beneficiary of the formula which was eventually to lead to his extraordinary success on radio, a formula so neatly explained in the title he chose for his celebrated radio series, *"Your Choice And Mine"*. He played for you what you wanted to hear, and then what you didn't know you wanted to hear, and having heard it, could hardly wait to hear it again.

Tommy, in that old world room in O'Connell Street, extracting a record from the hundreds which lined the walls and spilled out all over the house, even into the toilet: "I'm going to play you this little thing by Joseph Haydn".

One thing we both came to have very much in common - we both played the gramophone extremely well! He even conducted it with his battered old pipe, repaired in several places with sticking plaster. And sometimes, totally absorbed in the music, utterly relaxed, you might nearly fall out of your armchair when, unable to contain his own enthusiasm, he would screech out: "THERE'S GORGEOUS STRINGS!" or "JUST LISTEN TO THOSE TROMBONES!"

Those were days when journalism and music somehow got themselves inextricably interwoven until in an unexpected decision to retire from the newspaper fray he unravelled them in his own regard. "Tommy, are you really serious about retiring?" Tommy: "Sure what the hell would I be doing editing the Ballyporeen notes when I could be at home listening to Mozart!"

But in those days when Mozart and the District notes were all mixed up with one another, an Editor could kill a musical bird and a journalistic bird with one stone. There was this day way back in the fifties when the then Minister for Local Government, Mr. Neil T. Blaney, TD, invited us, in common with the other provincial papers, to a Press Conference at the Custom House in Dublin regarding the launching of a series of regional water supplies. It also happened that around the same time the current issue of *"The Gramophone"* carried a most laudatory review by its editor, Sir Compton Mackenzie, of a recently issued recording of the duet *"Home To Our Mountains"* from Verdi's *"Il Trovatore"*. The female half of the duet was the legendary contralto Ebe Stignani, a particular heroine of Tommy's and called by him "Eee Bee", and the male half was a hitherto unknown Italian tenor whose Christian name, as best I recall, was Mario and whose surname was either Bichi or Binchi. This Mario was hailed by Sir Compton as the greatest thing since Giovanni Martinelli, the tenor whom Tommy most

admired. This, of course, was a record that Tommy simply had to have and, having assigned me to confront Mr. Blaney at the Custom House, he nonchantly remarked in passing that as I would be in Dublin he might as well avail of my presence there to have me trot around to Mr. Moiselle's Gramophone Stores, in Johnson's Court off Grafton Street and purchase for him this recently issued and much lauded recording.

The nonchalance of the request belied the subsequent briefing. It seemed to have been taken for granted that I knew how to get to the Customs House (which I didn't), but the most meticulous instructions were given me on how to get to Grafton Street, identify Johnson's Court, the premises in question therein, and recognise Mr. Moiselle himself, for I was to do business with none other and was to make it clear to him for whom the record was being purchased. In case that did not put Mr. M. upon his mettle, I was told how to inspect the disk, clearing it of all possible flaws and faults before final acceptance.

No annointed of the Lord, bearing the sacrament of the sick, carried his privileged burden with more care and reverence than I bore the wrapped record of Mario and "Eee Bee" to the bus, into the train, changing at Ballybrophy and on down by Horse and Jockey, Faranaleen, Fethard and at last into Clonmel around 9 pm on a summer's evening. Scared? . . . If I broke it he'd kill me!

For all that, I had the temerity to endanger its safety by the addition of a further burden. I mean in those days it was unthinkable for a fellow to be in Dublin and not to return home laden with a copious supply of Haffner's sausages and puddings. And as the train slowed on its way through the Wilderness into Clonmel station, there was I, holding the record on my lap as if it were a bomb that might explode if it were even slightly stirred, but my eyes were contemplating with great anticipation the parcel of Haffners up on the luggage rack!

The truth of the matter was that between Neil Blaney, and Mario, (whatever his name was), I hadn't had time to have a decent meal all day, and I was starved with the hunger. I was greatly looking forward to speeding home for a fine feed. It was not to be! As I stepped from the train onto the platform among a goodly crowd of fellow travellers with a fair scattering there to meet them, a familiar stentorian voice for the top of the railway bridge hollered: "Brendan!" Everybody including me looked up. "Did you bring the record?", said he. I nodded weakly that indeed I had. Haffner's sausages how are you! He sped around to the station entrance to meet me, hands outstreched to rescue the record from my untrustworthy hands, and taking it from me with delicate reverence said: "Come on, we'll see now if he's as good as Sir Compton claims", and I was marched in a direction quite opposite to that which I had intended to go, wall-falling with the hunger into the Holy of Holies, the inner temple of the High Priest of the Gramophone.

I have never quite decided which, with Tommy, was the more elaborate ritual, the lighting of the pipe or the putting on of the record. The former ceremony, at any rate, was usually performed after accomplishing the latter. First then the shiny new disc, to which were committed the Verdian effusions of Mario and "Eee Bee", was extracted from its case with the air of an explosives expert diffusing a bomb. The freed recording, never held in any way that might involve the resting of even the shadow of a finger on the tracks, was then tilted this way and that under a side lamp to establish that it bore no flaws, and if it did , woe betide me!

Its mint condition then to my great relief thus established, a pad of felt was employed to give it a cleaning and polishing which it

clearly did not need, and there followed another minute of scrutiny of the surface before it was gingerly laid upon the gramophone turntable. "Now!" says the Maestro with the tone of a man who was not overwhelmed with confidence, "we'll see what Sir Compton's opinion is worth".

As the pickup is carefully lowered into the starting groove there is a cautionary "Whisht!" to me, even though I'm not making a sound. It is more warningly repeated as the moment arrives for Mario to introduce himself. He begins with a thoroughly agreeable "Se M'ami Anchor" and as he progresses with the introduction, the red of the pipe makes loops in the growing darkness for it has become a baton conducting the singer. From the baton wielder there comes a grunt of indeterminate mood leaving me uncertain whether the verdict so far is favourable or otherwise.

A plucking of strings to herald the entry of the contralto provokes another urgent "Whisht!" in my direction, I still as quiet as a mouse, and now it is Stignani's turn. The voice like liquid gold with an infinite and melting sadness pours forth and is almost immediately obscured in a sort of cry of ecstasy from the pipe wielding conductor immediately followed by a thunderous declaration in tones that I am sure can be heard up in the Comeraghs: "She's gorgeous!".

And then it was Mario's turn to come in with the exquisitely soothing and popular refrain "*Rest thee, O mother!*" He seemed to me to have a compelling lyrical quality, a bit thin perhaps but to be making a very commendable job of it, when I am caused to shoot in wild alarm out of my armchair by a cry of piercing anguish and unutterable outrage from the pipe wielder. Even as I am frantically reflecting if some intruder has stabbed him in the back, or if at least he has been overtaken by a most fearful onset of cramp he is bounding across the room and wresting the record from the turntable. The light is switched on and he is standing there glaring at me in angry disbelief, the record is held in his hand as if it is something infested with bubonic plague. In tones of a hushed and choking incredulity he says to me; "He took a breath!" And then, in case the enormity of this offence has not properly impressed itself on me, which it hadn't, he repeats in stentorian tones . . . "HE TOOK A BREATH!"

Alas poor Mario! Caruso, McCormack, Martinelli, Gigli and for that matter Frank Ryan and Tom Hogan could all sing that verse without pausing to take a breath. Taking a breath in that essential passage of "Home" just isn't done. But then didn't he always suspect that that Compton fellow hadn't a bloody clue what good singing was !

*Ebe Stignani - a particular heroine of Tommy's - "with a voice like liquid gold".*

The record so carefully purchased, so reverentially transported, so faithfully delivered, is contemptuously discarded in an atmosphere of outrage which adds to my gnawing hunger a quite unwarranted sense of creeping guilt. Have I now somehow been, however unwittingly, the instrument of polluting these hallowed shades with an outrageous insult to good music and good singing? Somehow, I cannot avoid the impression that there in the dock with Sir Compton and Mario is poor me, accessory before and after the fact. I diffidently suggest I should be going and am greatfully well underway when I have to go right back into the danger zone again - to rescue me Haffners' sausages!

Fashion in the sunshine at
Powerstown Park Races.

The band leads the competitors down the Western Road for the annual sports and (left) the parents came too in large numbers.

Even before Sean Kelly's era, there was a great interest in cycling locally, due in large measure to the enthusiasm of Bill Hyland, seen above (in cap) about to start another race.

Ladies walking races were all the go, with plenty of enthusiastic competitors (on opposite page), but the champions were the O'Keeffe sisters, with one of them winning yet again (above) at the finish at Kickham Barracks. Here too, Bill Hyland with stop watch at the ready, played a leading role.

Ballypatrick Tennis Tournament.

This was my one and only day spent shark fishing! I had joined Walter Smithwick (centre) from the Kilkenny brewing family for a day on the high seas out from Helvick Head. The blood from the two landed sharks brings back memories of seasickness - even after all these years.

*Cooling off in the Suir.*

A *boat just launched from the Workingmen's Boat Club sets off on its maiden voyage.*

ABOVE: *Ladies attending a Kilfeacle Beagles Day.*

LEFT: *Members of Clonmel Fencing Club.*

LEFT *and* ABOVE: *Tipperary Senior Hurlers and Croke Park action.*
BELOW: *Sportsfield winners.*

The funeral cortege of Lt. Col. P. J. Cunniffe, O.C. Kickham Barracks, passes the Munster Tribune offices in Parnell Street.

**Barney Cavanagh** *was one of the reporters on the new paper founded in 1955 in competition with* The Nationalist. *Here he recalls his early days in Clonmel with*

# The Munster Tribune

We came to fair Clonmel in midsummer 1955, Fintan Faulkner, Des Mullan and myself, as the editorial team setting up the *"Munster Tribune"* newspaper, with offices close by Hearn's Hotel and the Town Hall. Other young journalists joined later - Mick Strappe, Michael Hogan and Noel Smith. *The Tribune* was a lively weekly, with lots of pictures - and news on its front page which was unusual for Provincial papers of the time. It was seeking a share of readers alongside the long-established *Nationalist*, and succeeded too for a few years.

The paper was printed down at Davis Rd. by the *Sporting Press*, which of course also published the major greyhound newspaper of the time. The Directors included Arthur Morris, Sam King, James Clinton, Tommy O'Brien of the Ballingarry collieries and Des Hanafin.

On the commercial side were Noel Stapleton and later Billy Kenrick, labouring in the tough market of advertising. Most of the regular advertising went to the *Nationalist* with - in particular, several pages of auction announcements every week. The failure to attract this major advertising was to lead eventually to its demise and subsequent purchase by its rival up in Market St.

The Tribune *advertising reps, Billy Kenrick, seen here at the piano with popular Clonmel singer Sheila Cairns and (inset) Noel Stapleton.*

Noel Stapleton also carried on an insurance business in Mitchel St. and was a famous footballer with Clonmel Commercials as well as gaining a regular place on the county team. Billy Kenrick, who hailed from the Fethard area, won renown as a bandleader and before that, as one of Mick Delahunty's musicians. Around this time Billy became the proud father of twins, and appropriately would never fail to include in his dance repertoire, the hit tune of the time - *"Twenty Tiny Fingers"*, with the appropriate line:

> *"And the other one's got,*
> *a big bald spot,*
> *exactly like his pop"*!

I myself had "digs" in those days with the jovial Bridie and Joe Byrne up in Irishtown, and there were always a few fellow lodgers from Mick Del's Band. The strange thing was we seldom saw each other. The bandsmen travelled long distances every day in the wagon driven by Paddy Delahunty. Arriving back to Clonmel with the dawn, they would be gone again by mid-afternoon to provide the Glenn Miller music of *"Moonlight Serenade"*, *"American Patrol"* and all of the other favourites which made the orchestra the huge attraction it was for dancers all over the land and overseas.

*The Mick Delahunty Orchestra get ready on stage at the Tower Ballroom, before a Tipperary Golf Club Dance in 1955. The only female band member at this time was Eileen Sloan.*

Both Bridie and Joe Condon were lifelong members of the Pioneers and they are pictured here as members of the St. Mary's Branch (second from right centre row, with Bridie seated in front of him). They were also prominent members of the St. Mary's Choral Society, and I remember with great affection the Society's wonderful productions like "*Martha*" and the "*Lily of Killarney*" down in the Regal Theatre as well as a memorable train trip to Tralee for the Festival of Kerry. (See photographs in Frank Patterson's section of this book.) I recall in particular the performance of the stars of those shows including Tom Hogan, Nellie Corbett, Monica Cullen and Paddy Hickey.

Despite working for rival papers, we in *The Tribune* enjoyed a good working relationship with the editorial staff of *The Nationalist*, as we shared desks reporting on the County Council and Corporation meetings, court proceedings etc. Brendan Long and Edmond Symes were the senior reporters, together with Ted Dillon, Willie Fenton and Peggie Hickey who joined around this time. Willie Fenton was President of Hillview and is on the left of this picture taken at the 1955 Hillview Ball in the Collins Hall.

*The Nationalist* editor was father figure Willie Darmody. He had taken over the editor's chair from Tommy O'Brien, who was one of the town's great characters - although still not as nationally famous as he later became in subsequent years with his Radio Éireann programme, *"Your Choice and Mine"*. My impression is that there was "no love lost" between Tommy and the Nationalist Directors, for he readily agreed when Tribune editor Fintan Faulkner got him to write a racy column in which he regaled readers with his tall tales. Brendan Long has written his memory of Tommy elsewhere in this book

To be invited upstairs over "Mog" Condon's shop in O'Connell St., to listen to Tommy's latest collection of stereo recordings was a treat not to be missed. Stereo was a real novelty of the time when the norm was the 12 inch 78 rps disc. One of Tommy's records featuring the sounds of a steam train coming into a railway station amply demonstrated the attractions of this new recording technique - particularly when added to by an equally loud commentary from the man himself! He reviewed records for a number of newspapers and magazines around this time, and this no doubt brought a lot of the newer recordings his way for review purposes. His other great interest was mountain climbing, and he subsequently spent the closing years of his life in a house up the road to the Golf Club, where he was near his beloved Comeraghs.

Hillview Lawn Tennis and Pitch & Putt Club was a thriving sports and social club even in the fifties. Ernie Hogan was one of its leading members and also a member of the Clonmel Corporation where he was more ornately known as "E. O'Brien-Hogan".

He was a staunch defender of Fianna Fáil policy, and could more than hold his own in the many lively debates in the council chamber.

*Below: Ernie (seated centre) was President of Hillview when these prizes were awarded to the Pitch & Putt champions of that season.*

Also a leading member of the Hillview Club around this period was Jimmy Cummins (seated centre in above picture) who hailed from Kilkenny City. Jimmy was an army sergeant in Kickham Barracks, where I think he was the PE instructor. He was ever on hand for a bit of jollity.

His popularity was obvious from the crowds which gathered in the Collins Hall for his farewell presentation when he decided to leave Clonmel. I was there myself too that night (centre back row).

Also making a name for himself at this time on the local councils was a certain Sean Treacy. We, on the *Munster Tribune* liked to think that we helped to set him on the road to Dáil Éireann and greater fame as Ceann Comhairle.

Another memory of our days at the *Tribune* was that we were the first Irish newspaper to chronicle the initial success in the U.S.A. of the Clancy Brothers. The Clancys came, of course, from Carrick-on-Suir, joining up with Tommy Makem from Keady in Co. Armagh to form the first of the great ballad groups of the '50s.

*The Tribune's* correspondent in Carrick was Frank O'Driscoll, then a lively and hard working local government official. But he could

equally have been a very successful journalist, for his Carrick notes and news in the *Tribune* were a great attraction. It was Frank who informed us of the early success of the Clancys in New York, but even he could not have imagined that the Clancys would still be singing, almost un-changed, around the world forty years later. Peg Power of Carrick music and drama fame was a sister of the Clancys - surely one of the greatest Tipperary families of the century.

Another story from the *Tribune* days, happened when I was sent to Ballyporeen to cover - as far as I remember, the official opening of an extension to a school. This was long before the Hollywood actor of local descent had any thoughts of the White House in Washington, and who would make the village internationally known one day by his Presidential visit!

Anyway after the opening, John Boyle, a County Councillor from the Ardfinnan area, suggested I should meet a group of local women who had gathered to watch the ceremony. "There's one here you might like to meet" he said, as he introduced me to an oldish woman dressed entirely in black. "This is Katie Ryan" he said. True enough she confirmed she was the lady made famous in the John McCormack classic "*The Fairy Tree*" from the poem written by Temple Lane and set to music by McCormack's singing teacher Dr. Vincent O'Brien.

LEFT:
*Frank O'Driscoll.*

RIGHT:
*John Boyle.*

## 'Fairy tree' link won her renown

By BERNARD CAVANAGH
IRISH PRESS Reporter

Eighty seven - years - old Katie Ryan of Clogheen, Co. Tipperary, who has died in a Cashel hospital, was identified as the Katie Ryan in the song, "The Fairy Tree."

*"But Katie Ryan saw there in some sweet dream she had,*
*The Blessed Son of Mary, and oh His face was sad"* . . .

Katie told me she had no idea why the author had mentioned her in the verses, but a few years later, when working in Dublin for the *Irish Press*, I managed to track down the author. *"Temple Lane"* was a pseudonym for Isabel Leslie, living then in Dun Laoghaire.

I spoke to her on the phone, but never got a chance to meet her. She told me that as a young girl she and her sister often spent holidays in the Clogheen area. Her father was a Church of Ireland clergyman. Although she had never met Katie Ryan, she felt she must have been told about her as a local character, and had written her into the verse.

By a strange coincidence, around the time I met Katie Ryan in Ballyporeen, there was a young Clonmel lad playing a lively game of tennis up at Hillview, and eyeing the girls all the while. His name was Frank Patterson, and at the time he was showing no interest in song. Now if he had ever met Katie Ryan, he might have made something of it!

# THE MUNSTER Tribune

Vol. 4. No. 46.  FRIDAY, SEPTEMBER 5, 1958  PRICE 3d.

Tipp. Weddi Group

Picture at the Galtee Hotel, Cahir, on Wednesday, shows Mr. Derek McNulty, Grove St., Roscrea, and Miss Mary Tuohy, Barronstown, Tipperary, and guests after their wedding at St. Michael's Church, Tipperary. Best man was Lieut. T. McNulty, Portobello Barracks, and Miss Phyllis Flaherty, cousin of the bride, was bridesmaid. The ceremony, with Nuptial Mass and Papal Blessing, was performed by Rev. D. Costelloe, P.P., Monaggea, Newcastlewest, assisted by Rev. J. Morrissey, P.P., Kilteely, and Rev. M. A. O'Dwyer, C.C., Tipperary.

## A Fair Exchange

## Welcome For Tipp's New Town Clerk

INTRODUCING their new Town Clerk, Mr. Richard I. McCarthy, to the members of Tipperary Urban Council on Monday night, Councillor T. K. O'Donoghue, Chairman, said he was very glad to welcome their new man to the town.

He hoped the affairs of the Council would be run well under his direction. They were all sorry to lose the last man, Mr. Kirby, who had given great service.

Mr. McCarthy returned thanks for the welcome and said: "I hope you will not have anything to complain about."

A native of Cork, Mr. McCarthy took up his new position as Town Clerk on Monday morning. Before coming to Tipperary he was Town Clerk in Kinsale. At Murphy's Hotel, Kinsale, last week, Mr. McCarthy received a presentation from the members of Kinsale Urban Council. Mr. John Barrett, Chairman of the Council, who made the presentation of a notes, said he had lic officials in met be

## They May Make Up Their Minds This Week

Some members of South Tipperary County Council are apparently unable to make up their minds as to what day of the week they should hold their meetings. For a considerable time past, the meetings had been held on Monday, as is the general practice all over the country, but number of members pres a change, as he was unsuitable g. last

## His Age Saved Him From Jail

"You are 74 years of age but if you were any your uld be sent to jai Skinner at D nesday

Just O Light All The Want

The people of Toem three miles from Cappa have a request for Sou perary County Council. would like the Council to public light in the middl village. They claim thei light erected when lig erected at some cross-road there are no shops at all. And the points in favo erection of the light are: lage had over 40 residents, four shops, and it is hope two more shortly; the villa uated on a much used pu which has a bus service.

Gone Back New Yor

RIGHT: The start of the hunting season was always a great day in Fethard's Main Street. Mrs. Croome-Carroll, together with her six daughters and their ponies made a unique family group.

ABOVE: The local bank manager (on left with pipe) came out to see the move-off.

TOP RIGHT: She probably would not have joined the Hunt, but was happy to take part in a fancy dress competition on the Green at Ardfinnan.

RIGHT: "Field Days" were popular in the 'fifties. They usually included displays of farm produce, machinery and show-jumping competitions. This one was in Killenaule.

BELOW: They attended an I.C.A. Federation meeting in Cashel.

BELOW RIGHT: Work in progress on new church at Rathcormack.

OPPOSITE PAGE: Not all members of the Irish Countrywomen's Association lived in the rural areas. This group, pictured in the Tower Ballroom, were from the Tipperary Town Guild.

RIGHT: Nearby in Bansha is gathered the Committee of the local Agricultural Show.

ABOVE: Members of the Mullinahone Show Committee.

RIGHT: Joe Rea (extreme right standing) had a keen interest in Cahir Macra na Feirme long before he became a national figure in farming activities.

When Dr. Thomas Morris was ordained Archbishop of Cashel and Emly, there was justifiable pride in his native Killenaule. I had attended his consecration ceremony in Thurles Cathedral, and was there too for his homecoming to the village church some weeks later.

RIGHT: The organising committee of the "Welcome Home" ceremonies.

BELOW RIGHT: The altar boys who took part in the ceremony.

Dr. Morris, as Archbishop of Cashel and Emly, was also Patron of the G.A.A., and in this capacity I had occasion to visit him in Thurles, where he always had time for a chat and a cup of tea. He readily agreed to my request for an interview with Kathleen Watkins at Holycross when we featured the magnificent restoration of the Abbey in a "Faces & Places" programme.

OPPOSITE PAGE: The annual Liam Lynch commemoration ceremonies near the Vee above Clogheen was well attended by the ladies on this occasion.

Roisín O'Donnell (left in photo on right) was an excellent singer as well as being able to display her ballet skills as she does here with some of her fellow participants before a performance in Cashel's City Hall.

153

OPPOSITE PAGE: *The Marian Grotto is a familiar sight on the Clonmel-Dungarvan Road - just beyond Ballymacarberry. This is my picture of the ceremonies on the day it was unveiled almost 40 years ago.*

RIGHT *and* BELOW: *Confirmation Day at Kilcash and Kilsheelan.*

155

Teacher Sean Carew and pupils with Fr. Carey, when he revisited his old school at Marlfield, following his ordination to the priesthood.

ABOVE: Kilsheelan pupils pictured following the opening of their new school.

RIGHT: Pupils of Grange school out at Knocklofty.

*The boys from SS. Peter & Paul's who were Confirmed in 1960.*

*How many of these names can you match to the faces in the picture (opposite page)?*

| | | |
|---|---|---|
| Brian | Ahearne | Gladstone St. |
| Johnny | Arrigan | Cashel Rd. |
| Ted | Bowe | Northfields |
| John | Brady | Plunkett Trce. |
| Paddy | Brady | Plunkett Trce. |
| Paddy | Branigan | Baron Park |
| Pat | Brett | Old Waterford Rd. |
| Peter | Browne | Baron Park |
| Herbert | Buck | Garrymore |
| Ciaran | Burke | Old Bridge |
| P.J. | Burke, R.I.P. | Davitt Ave. |
| Liam | Butler | Griffith Ave. |
| Brothers | Byrne | Plunkett Trce. |
| Kevin | Byrne | Baron Park |
| Billy | Cahill | Thomas St. |
| Padge | Carey | Gladstone St. |
| Sean | Carroll | Árd Fatima |
| Connie | Carroll | Árd Fatima |
| Michael | Casey | William St. |
| Liam | Cooney | Baron Park |
| Billy | Cooney | Old Bridge |
| Jim | Corbett | Griffith Ave. |
| Johnny | Coyne | Mountain Rd. |
| Michael | Cunningham | Kickham St. |
| Anthony | Dempsey | Davis Rd. |
| Frank | Doolan | Griffith Ave. |
| Pat | Fahey | Mountain Rd. |
| Michael | Farrell | Slievenamon Rd. |
| Noel | Farrell | Slievenamon Rd. |
| Pat | Fitzgerald | Árd Na Greine |
| Noel | Gardiner | Cross St. |
| Seamus | Gregory | Duckett St. |
| Arthur | Gregory | Duckett St. |
| Liam | Griffin R.I.P. | Thomas St. |
| John | Hackett | Árd Na Greine |
| Anthony | Hahessy | Morton St. |
| Mossie | Hally | Garrymore |
| Pat | Hartigan | College St. |
| Jimmy | Healy | Davis Rd. |
| Peter | Hopkins | Garrymore |
| Seamus | Kavanagh | Griffith Ave. |
| Jim | Kelliher | Árd Na Greine |
| Anthony | Kerton | Fr. Matthew Trce. |
| Ritchie | Kiely | Plunkett Trce. |
| Gabriel | Lacey | Davitt Ave. |
| Michael | Landers | College St. |
| John | Lawless | Kilganey |
| Jackie | Lawlor | Mountain Rd. |
| Alec | Logue | Baron Park |
| Robert | Logue | Baron Park |
| Paul | Lonergan | Davitt Ave. |
| Johnny | Lonergan | Garrymore |
| Liam | Maher | James St. |
| Stephen | Mackey | Griffith Ave. |
| Christy | Maguire | Sheehy Trce. |
| Frank | McCormack | Griffith Ave. |
| Denis | McDonagh | Emmet St. |
| Pat | McGrath | Slievenamon Rd. |
| Noel | Meaney | Fr. Matthew Trce. |
| Thomas | Moroney | Sheehy Trce. |
| Eamon | Mullins | Slievenamon Rd. |
| Noel | Murphy | Árd Na Greine |
| Noel | Murray | Árd Na Greine |
| Paddy | Nagle | Baron Park |
| Jim | Nolan | Dillon St. |
| Tom | O'Brien | Mountain Rd. |
| Michael | O'Brien | Mountain Rd. |
| Jimmy | O'Brien | Slievenamon Rd. |
| Martin | O'Brien | Mary St. |
| Tim | O'Brien | Davis Rd. |
| Tommy | O'Brien | Parnell St. |
| Tommy | O'Brien | Griffith Ave. |
| Gerry | O'Donoghue | Davitt Ave. |
| Peter | O'Donoghue | Davitt Ave. |
| Paddy | O'Donoghue | Thomas St. |
| Pat | O'Donoghue | College St. |
| Christy | O'Dwyer | Davis Rd. |
| Frank | O'Keeffe | King's Close |
| Jimmy | O'Neill | Parnell St. |
| Paud | O'Reilly | Queen St. |
| Michael | Ó Suilleabháin | Mitchel St. |
| Noel | Patterson | Árd Na Greine |
| Junior | Pollard | King St. |
| Billy | Power | Griffith Ave. |
| Larry | Power | Griffith Ave. |
| Tom | Power | Davitt Ave. |
| Seanie | Power | Plunkett Trce. |
| Christy | Poyntz | Dillon St. |
| Kevin | Prendergast | Old Bridge |
| Paddy | Purcell | Davitt Ave. |
| Tony | Pyke | Kickham St. |
| Con | Ryan | Baron Park |
| Donal | Ryan | Giantsgrave |
| Noel | Shanahan | Árd Na Greine |
| Michael | Slattery | Emmet St. |
| Norris | Teddy | River St. |
| Liam | Tobin | Griffith Ave. |
| P.J. | Tobin | Davitt Ave. |
| Michael | Voulkes | Cashel Rd. |
| Joe | White | Griffith Ave. |
| Michael | Woods | Emmet St. |

In Feb. '96 The Nationalist *published the photo (see page* 158) *so that the boys could be identified.* **James O'Brien** *was able to identify* 103 *of his colleagues* 36 *years later and writes this account of:*

# Confirmation Day 1960 at SS. Peter & Paul's, Clonmel

Looking at this group of over 100 boys who were confirmed in SS. Peter & Paul's by Bishop Russell, it would be difficult to compare the achievements of each individual over the past 36 years as a number now run their own businesses - at least one is now a doctor, one a university professor, and many are employed in State companies. However, probably the best known nationally is musician Michael Ó Suileabháin (3rd from right 2nd row), who is now head of music at University College, Limerick. It is estimated about a dozen of my colleagues from that Confirmation Day of 1960, now live abroad.

Great changes have taken place in the town since our school days. One of the busiest areas then was around the railway station. There were two main lines then. In addition to the existing Limerick-Waterford line, there was also the Dublin line via Thurles. This line was particularly busy on match days -particularly on the Munster Hurling final day in Thurles when "Specials" would be carrying hundreds of Clonmel supporters, stopping at Fethard, Farnaleen, Laffansbridge and Horse and Jockey before arriving at Thurles.

Old Clonmel character Jackie Dalton would be there selling fruit and chocolate from his

basket both at the station and on the train, while John Blake would shout "Hats and Colours of the game"! This was the era before the diesel engines, and what a sight it was to see two steam engines coupled together pulling a large number of carriages. Jack Dunphy was usually the driver of such steam engines. Unlike to-day's diesel trains, the steam engines had to be turned around at the station. This was done by means of a turntable which was situated about a quater of a mile from the main platform.

A large amount of goods and merchandise was delivered to business houses in Clonmel from the station by means of horse drawn floats. A big shire horse pulled each float, and daily they could be seen trekking around the town delivering the goods. At lunch time each day, Bill Lafford would tie his horse to the railings of his dwelling at Fr. Matthew Trce., and while enjoying his own meal would keep an eye out the window on his "charge" enjoying a nosebag of oats. These lovely animals were similiar to the ones seen to-day in the Budweisser TV ads, or pulling the Royal coaches at the Sandown Park race meeting in April.

Just around the corner from Bill's house was a small industry which was to mushroom into one of the flagships of employment in the town, namely Showerings - known then as Bulmers. The timber crates of Woodpecker cider were mounted high around the factory grounds, and the clinking of the bottles could be heard for quite a distance all around. Factory manager Dan O'Mahony kept a watchful eye on the proceedings.

The Princess Garage and Bus Depot - now Larry O'Keeffe's, was a thriving enterprise which ran a daily

bus service to Thurles and also Sunday excursions to Tramore.

Prendergast's Garage across the road was Clonmel's biggest, being the main Ford Dealer. Next door Bill Purcell's cycle shop was also a leader in its field. Back across the road again , Kickham Army Barracks has changed little in the intervening years. One remembers Sunday mornings in particular when the soldiers would parade impressively around the square, to the commands of men like Srgt. Major Joe Browne who was also a leading member of Clonmel's Fencing Club (see photo page 136).

Just below the Regal and opposite the barracks was the Showgrounds or "Carnival field" as it was sometimes called. A popular sport of the time were the walking races which usually ended around the field, coinciding with the start of a travelling carnival or circus. The O'Keeffe Sisters (see page 130) and George Moss were the champion walkers in those days.

One particularly memorable circus to pitch here was the occasion when Chipperfield's brought along no fewer than twelve elephants (a photo of their arrival off a special train up at the railway station is included elsewhere in this book), a giraffe, and many other exotic animals, to perform in a 4,000 seater big top (see page 54).

Another unforgettable feature of the times was the Fair Days in Clonmel. (See photo page 9). The Mall was one of the main areas where the wooden stalls were set up, with O'Connell St. too getting a share of the activity. It would be hard to picture O'Connell St. to-day with wooden stalls erected on the footpaths into which the cattle were placed while the bargaining continued. At about 5 p.m. when the fair had ended, the footpaths and roadway would be awash with organic manure until each shopkeeper would clean the footpath outside his own premises. Strangely nobody complained as the fair brought good business to the town.

Moving up Parnell St., the Ritz Cinema, which is now the Credit Union, housed huge crowds at this time before the arrival of television. Corbett's Printing was another busy enterprise while across the road Bobby O'Brien's Bakery supplied confectionery to a large number of shops in the town. King and Keating's Garage (now Quirke's Furniture) were the main Austin dealers, and farther up the street past Hearn's Hotel was Sloan's clothes store where

one could buy on the instalment system. A catch-phrase of the time was - "Sloan's?" This was used when someone was seen wearing a new coat, and real Clonmel people would know the meaning of the catchphrase.

Another popular outfitters was the Blackrock Store at the corner of Mitchel St. and Abbey St. Here the children were treated to a free ride on a big timber rocking horse, and of course a visit to Santa there at Christmas time was a must. One couldn't leave Mitchel St. without a mention of "Hogan's Hotel" which is now the Harp Bar. Down in Abbey St. opposite the Friary many people bought their first record or musical gear in Belynda Cashin's record store.

Arriving at the Main Guard, Cooney's Shop and Bar (page 170) was a hive of activity. For a generation kindly John Ahearne weighed out tea and sugar while chatting to his wide range of customers both urban and rural. His generous disposition will never be forgotten by those who knew him. Leaving Cooneys, the two busiest streets of the town were at right angles. Straight ahead was "Bradio for Radio" while across the street was McCreery's impressive furniture store which had been rebuilt following a disastrous fire (see page 34).

Mae Lonergan's greengrocer shop was another jewel. "Good morning Denis", Mae would say to Denis Burke, a former Mayor, Senator and well know businessman as he made his way to his bacon shop further up the street.

But the mecca of all stores had to be Woolworths half way up O'Connell St. Dunnes or any other of the big stores of to-day couldn't compare to "Woolies" (see page 16). From the moment you entered through the big doors where a large "stand-on" weighing scales stood, you were entering a fascinating shop where virtually everything was sold. Originally the Woolworths stores' motto was that nothing cost more than a "tanner" or about two and a half pence in to-day's money. On Christmas Eve it was almost impossible to even get into the store, so large were the crowds. The Co-Op bakery and the Home and Colonial were also well supported but they all seemed very dull after leaving Woolworths.

RIGHT: *O'Connell Street with Woolworths in centre of photo.*

BELOW RIGHT: *Lalor's Drapery Shop in the background as Rás Tailteann riders flash past.*

BELOW LEFT: *Cooney's Shop at the Main Guard.*

Back in Gladstone St., the Ormonde Hotel (see page 53) was the place to dine. John Joe Murphy immaculately dressed in his porter's uniform politely directed the guests. Lowry's Hardware across the road, (now the ACC building) had an overhead cash/receipt system which left the children spellbound as they watched the money their parents had tendered travel overhead to the cash office, and their change and receipt would be returned via the same route. Around the corner in Market St. were the old Nationalist Offices with the Collins Hall across the road with Wallace's Garage and a wool store on either side.

*Fr. Meehan with the Boys' Club Committee.*

Another important facet of Clonmel life around this time was the Pipe Band. Anthony Fennessey led the way and the music could be heard for miles around. They were based in the Boys' Club in Sarsfield St. under the guidance of Fr. William Meehan C.C. who also ran a very successful amateur juvenile boxing club.

Summer holidays in Clonmel were spent swimming either in the Suir or in the Anner. Trips to the "Wilderness" along the Dublin railway line, and a visit to the "Giant's Rock" up at the "Wildy" will bring back many happy memories to children of this era. The Frenchman's stream (now Glenpatrick Spring) was also popular where brickeens by the jarful could be caught with cabbage strainers!

Hundreds of children would have had little in the way of pocket money were it not for Bulmers who employed large numbers picking blackcurrants at Redmondstown and Annerville. Gerry Coffey, the farm manager would ensure that all of the trees were picked bare and for hundreds of children it brought them their first pay packets. A good picker could earn up to £4 per week - a tidy sum in the late fifties.

Work at this time was hard to come by and many men and indeed whole families travelled to England in search of work. A phrase one didn't want to hear was the "Boat-train". Many Clonmel families were glad of the registered letter containing cash sent by family members from abroad each week. Main employers in the town were Currans, the Pram factory and Munster Shoes.

Finally a few other shops alas no longer in business which will jog some memories - The "Favourit" coffee shop, Charlie Carri's Bar with the big "Time Beer" bottle painted high on the front of the wall at the corner of Dillon St., Alyward's Wholesale, Sargeant's Sweetshop, Boyd Ryans, Waldrons, Whites, Suttons Coalyard, Morans, Imco Cleaners, Arthur Powers, Clonmel Drapery and Lalors (see photo on previous page).

Another of the boys in that Confirmation group was **Joe White** who is now living in England. He recalls those:

# Golden Days

Looking at myself smiling out from the middle of the fourth row from the back on page 158, surrounded by so many familiar faces, many of them long forgotten, certainly transported my mind back to those heady days of seemingly endless Summers and bitterly cold winters of so long ago.

School was SS. Peter & Paul's C.B.S. - "The Brothers" and more affectionately known as "The Old School" with Bro. O'Grady ("Charlie") at the helm. He had the ability to strike fear into our little hearts by the merest glance in our direction. Then there was Liam Walsh with his renowned "grainey-up" (but what a superb teacher) and Bro. Moloney who seemed to be a giant of a man, threatening us with the dreaded "bridge of asses". Isn't it amazing how we remember the few negatives, when there was so much good?

I vividly remember Bro. Dunne, who produced and directed our three-in-a-row Ceol Drama wins in the annual Feile Cluain Meala in the late 'fifties (see photo above right), pleading with us in the Regal Theatre to take, and keep, achievements such as these as our abiding memories of our schooldays. How right he was.

ABOVE: *Féile Cluain Meala winners in the Regal.*

BELOW: *"The School Around the Corner" was a favourite with radio listeners before it successfully transferred to television.*

Ireland, and the McCarthy Cup being paraded from the railway station to the Town Hall; the air full of jigs and reels as the Lane Band (see page 88) played outside the High School as we made our way home in the evenings; picking blackberries up by the Ragwell; collecting mushrooms in "Nosey" Purcell's wilderness; fishing for brickeens in the Frenchers and dudding apples from various orchards, (and getting caught!) to mention but a few.

Clonmel was also a hive of activity sportswise, with matches every week in the GAA sportsfield up on the Western Rd., to which we flocked, especially to see anybody playing against the Swans, upon you could always depend for a good fight - even if the game was poor!

I remember serving Mass for Fr. Lane, who was far ahead of his time in bringing the Church to us, the children of the town, at our own level. He never spoke down to us, nor did he dictate, but he was the first priest to encourage open discussion on equal terms, allowing us our point of view, and discouraging the then standard practise of touching one's forelock when meeting one of the Clergy. A great man of God. Ar dheis De go raibh a anam.

Summer memories recall a myriad of cameos, including swimming at the Green (see page 134), collecting brochures and "freebies" - such as they were, at the Horse Show, Tipperary winning the All-

The town was one of the country's cycling capitals, thanks to Bill Hyland (seated centre at a cycling club dinner), with big races all year round, attracting the superstars of the sport like Kerry's Gene Mangan, and our own heroes like Tommy Whelan; the Kiely brother - Tom and "Chops"; the "Ballina Bullet" - Mickey Slattery and the outstanding Johnny Gearon (see page 128). It was many a Sunday afternoon we sat on the kerb outside Bill's house on the Davis road, watching what we later came to know as the peleton, flashing past each time they completed a lap of the Colville Road - Carrick circuit, and crowded around the finish line as they made the sprint accompanied by a running commentary over a loudspeaker by Bill.

With the onset of Autumn and Winter, the pungent aroma of apples being crushed by Bulmers in Dowd's Lane enveloped the town for a few weeks every year; the Boulick stream always overflowed, turning Jock Carroll's field into a lake and later into the biggest ice rink in the area. We gathered chestnuts in Gortnafluir, selected the best and put them in the range oven to harden them up for the annual conker contests. Pouring basins full of water down the hill in Griffith Avenue, where I lived, so that we had our own Crista Run when it froze. The highlight, of course, as I'm sure it still is today, was the Santa Claus Express, every Christmas Eve, as it made its way from Irishtown to Ferryhouse. We used to stand waiting for it in O'Connell Street for hours, and follow it as far as the Kickham Barracks, where the Army would put on a fireworks display.

The late 'fifties also brought to Clonmel, a revival of the 1st and 4th Tipp. Troops of the C.B.S.I. Scout movement under the direction of Michael Drohan and Christy Browne. This was a tremendous boost for the young boys of the town, and I am pleased to note that it is still thriving today. I can still smell the

sausages sizzling over twig fires, and taste the tea made from the stream water in Glenary where we went on Sunday hikes.

Fair Days were great fun, especially in the later afternoon when the local Fire Brigade hosed down O'Connell Street and Gladstone Street after the cattle were gone and the wooden barriers had been removed from the shop windows. It was many a time we arrived home soaked through.

In those pre television times, our great escape to fantasy lay in the towns two cinemas - The Ritz and the Oisin, where the matinees on Saturdays and Sundays for an admission price of 10d downstairs or a shilling for the balcony, had both places bulging at the seams, and from which we emerged, hoarse and sweating, having cheered every gallant deed of our heroes of the screen. (See Edmond Symes story on Clonmel's Cinemas).

I don't know if it was exclusive to Clonmel, but another practice from then was Comic Swapping. Once you accumulated a bundle of comics which you had read - be they the weekly *Dandy*, *Beano* etc., or the more expensive *Dells*, D.C's, "64 Page" or "68 page" you would head off to knock on the doors of your friends homes to swap them for fresh issues. I can assure you that the bartering which took place in this pursuit engendered keen negotiating skills in my generation of townspeople.

They were simple, uncomplicated times, full of innocence and fun, where Clonmel was our universe, where anything that happened outside the town seemed to be of little, if any, consequence to us, and where we had the advantage of being brought up in an environment of love, protection and security.

Golden days indeed.

*Another Confirmations group at SS. Peter & Paul's. This time from 1959.*

ABOVE: Dave Hurley was the Chief Agricultural Officer for South Tipperary who regularly wrote informative articles on farming matters for The Nationalist which I would be required to illustrate. He is pictured above with his wife and children at a baby show in Powerstown Park.

LEFT: Some familiar Clonmel faces of the 'fifties.

One of the town's well known landmarks - the Main Guard.

A sunny Gladstone Street with the Comeragh Foothills adding to the scene.

*Tennis winners at Davis Road.*

Presentation Convent pupils.

LEFT: Mother and baby make a happy picture at a baby show in Powerstown Park.

RIGHT: *I climbed up the Comeragh foothills to record the storm-damaged Holy Year Cross.*

174

LEFT: Fr. Cyril (centre) during construction of the St. Anthony's Shrine at the Friary, caused quite a controversy by replacing all of the Church windows (top right opposite page) with modern coloured glass.

ABOVE: On their way to St. Patrick's Well during the St. Patrick's Day celebrations.

LEFT: Marching on St. Patrick's Day. What a lovely cap!

BELOW: Fr. Bracken, while curate in Ballymacarberry, could always be relied on to produce winning musical groups such as these pictured following Féile Cluain Meala. While his sister Molly (top left picture on opposite page) was a very successful art teacher in Clonmel.

OPPOSITE PAGE:

Top right: Enjoying the party at Lisronagh.

Bottom left: Members of the O'Meara School in another of their successful stage productions.

Bottom right: Colm Ó Cleirigh helps with the make-up before the "Pirates of Penzance" musical in the Loreto Convent.

ABOVE: *They attended a St. Mary's Choral Society Social.*

LEFT: *Competitors in a Kilsheelan I.C.A. Fancy Dress Competition.*

OPPOSITE PAGE - *Top: Tennis winners at the Island Club.*

*Right: "The Mothers' Party" was always a jolly occasion in the Sisters of Charity Hall in Morton Street.*

*Below: They helped make Burke's prize-winning sausages.*

RIGHT: Joan Denise Moriarty did an enormous amount to develop ballet skills in Munster in particular. Her her own troupe performed in the Regal Theatre and she held classes in the Collins Hall where she is pictured with some of her pupils.

ABOVE and RIGHT: More happy faces at the Military Ball in Kickham Barracks.

ABOVE: Yet more evidence of Fr. Bracken's musical guidance, this time pictured on the Green at Ardfinnan.

LEFT: Miss O'Meara's school was terrific for all sorts of action songs, dancing and even puppeteering as shown by this group who were also winners at Féile Cluain Meala.

ABOVE: Ted Young receives his trophy at Hillview.

BELOW: A group of teachers on the occasion of the retirement of one of their members, Mrs. Ó Cleirigh.

ABOVE: The future Ceann Comhairle Sean Treacy together with the Mayor Michael Kilkelly were among this group from Clonmel who took part in a social study conference at Mount Melleray.

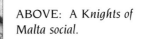

ABOVE: A Knights of Malta social.

LEFT: When Denis Hickey (centre front row) decided to emigrate to the U.S.A. a large gathering of his friends and sporting colleagues gave him a great farewell party in the Collins Hall.

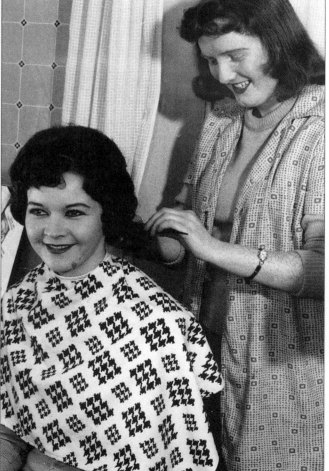

LEFT: Members of Clonmel Post Office staff at a retirement party for one of their colleagues while (below left) more Post Office staff pictured at their annual staff dinner in Kilcoran Lodge.

BELOW: Eithne Maher puts the final touches to another hair creation in her salon.

ABOVE: Valerie Burke and Alice McCormack with their colleagues from a Loreto Convent production.

ABOVE RIGHT: Boys from the High School on a visit to Kickham Barracks.

RIGHT: They attended a teeangers hop in the Collins Hall.

LEFT: *They were all prizewinners in the Sportsfield on the Western Road.*

BELOW: *First Holy Communion Class in the Loreto Convent.*

OPPOSITE PAGE:

Top Left: *The Loreto Convent hockey team who had just won a tournament.*

Bottom Left: *The senior girls in the Presentation Convent. Mary Slattery (second from left front row) became one of the earliest female assistant managers with A.I.B.*

The Ceann Comhairle was elected Mayor of Clonmel on two occasions.

ABOVE LEFT: He receives his chain of office from Matt Slater.

BELOW LEFT: The members of the Corporation join him with the County Manager P. J. Flynn and Town Clerk J. V. Nolan.

ABOVE: Mayor Treacy receiving another visitor at the Town Hall.

ABOVE RIGHT: Labhras Ó Murchú, who is Director General of Comhaltas Ceoltóirí Éireann, has hidden acting talents as we can see from his inclusion (back left) in this group from the Cashel Dramatic Society!

TOP LEFT: Competitors at a High School sports.

LEFT: Enjoying themselves at a Badminton Club social.

LEFT:
*High School pupils before setting off to the Gaeltacht.*

RIGHT:
*Pupils of Newtown-anner National School with their teachers.*

The two girls on right were winners in a Beauty Competition held in the County Ballroom, Cashel, while the three Clonmel ladies above, together with Bebe Moran (right) could also have been in the running for the title.

Half of the town's population would appear to have been members of the Pioneers' Total Abstinence Association. This is just a section of the attendance at a rally in Irishtown.

*Raymond Smith is quite an authority on book publishing with many titles to his credit - the most recent being "Urbe Et Orbi and All That". He provided me with useful guidance when I began this project, and also remembers there were two Tommy O'Briens:*

# "Tommy Coal" and "Tommy Ceoil"

There was another Tommy O'Brien in Clonmel apart from the man who became a national institution from his popular radio programme, which gave so much pleasure to so many and helped popularise Opera throughout Ireland.

I refer, of course, to the Tommy O'Brien, who was known as "Tommy Coal" or "The Coalminer" (back right in above photo). Born in County Mayo, he had come back in the 'Fifties from England, where he had gained ample experience of mining and re-opened the Ballingarry mines in South Tipperary. By dint of hard work and a real go-go attitude, he proved that a local area could be resuscitated in an era of depressing emigration. He had soon turned it into a going concern, giving good employment in the locality.

He never asked anyone to do something that he couldn't do himself. Once he had a strike on his hands in the Ballingarry mines for increased wages. He told the men that production wasn't high enough to merit it. "If you can take out as much as I

can in a day, then I'll pay you more than what you're getting at present", he told them. So he went down the mine and took out so much on the day that it was impossible for any of the men to take him on in his challenge.

Once a visitor to Clonmel stopped his car in the centre of the town to seek directions to Tommy O'Brien's house and a wit, standing at the street corner, asked him: "Do you mean 'Tommy Coal' or 'Tommy Ceoil'?".

On Ireland's racetracks and at Cheltenham and other English racecourses also, Tommy O'Brien was known and recognised as one of the most fearless gamblers of his time. By today's money values, some of his most spectacular wins and losses were absolutely astounding.

He returned from Cheltenham in 1960 with winnings totalling £30,000. I checked with the Economics Department of the Central Bank to ascertain what that would represent today and the answer came back £385,240.

There are few episodes in the history of great racing gambles to compare with his bid to clear £100,000 on the 1960 Champion Hurdle on his own horse Moss Bank - and, remember, that by today's values that would have been equivalent to taking £1 million out of the ring, if he succeeded. So certain was Tommy O'Brien of bringing off the coup that he had booked a luxury cruise for his wife Mary and himself in the immediate aftermath of the Cheltenham meeting.

Wearing the familiar O'Brien Cross of Lorraine colours, Moss Bank had to swerve to avoid Albergo when he fell at the second last. He was eating up the ground at the finish but was beaten three lengths by the 4/1 shot, Eborneezer, trained by Ryan Price and ridden by Fred Winter. Tommy O'Brien went ahead with the luxury cruise and got Michael O'Hehir to back Antirrhinum for him at the Baldoyle St. Patrick's Day meeting. The winnings came close to £50,000.

Tommy O'Brien was such a compulsive gambler that he didn't know when to stop. One day at the Curragh he was £22,000 ahead but an hour later he had fallen £30,000 behind - a turnover of over £50, 000. Awesome is the only word to describe it. Compare the scale of his betting with the fact that at this time I had come under his wing as Editor of *The Munster Tribune*, which he had established in opposition to *The Nationalist*, also printed in Clonmel and two other papers in the county, *The Tipperary Star* and *The Nenagh Guardian*.

I was appointed at £17.50 a week and along with that was covering the dogs at Clonmel and Kilkenny for "*The Sporting Press*" and also doing doggy tips for "*The Sunday Review*". In all I was earning £25 a week and it seemed beneath my dignity to go into ordinary "digs"! I did a deal with Hearne's Hotel (pictured on right) along with a few more of the bachelor set. We had bed and breakfast and a steak in the evening for £7.50 a week. But if you think that was paradise on earth, you have got to remember that the starting salary for a reporter from the provinces, arriving in one of the Dublin papers in 1960 was £13.50 a week.

Hearnes Hotel was just across the road from "*The Munster Tribune*". I didn't exactly stroll across to work carrying a rolled umbrella. You wouldn't last long in Clonmel or Thurles or in any part of County Tipperary for that matter if you adopted airs and graces and tried to "put on act", as they liked to say. I had been grounded in a knowledge of hurling over ten years on *The Tipperary*

*Star*, after finishing my schooling in that great nursery of the national game, Thurles C.B.S. As a local reporter, you covered the entire "beat", which meant that you did not confine yourself to sport alone but you had to cover as well meetings of the Urban Council and the County Council, the courts and write obituaries and, in a word, put your hand to a whole range of tasks. As you grew in experience, you learned how to plan and lay out a page and edit on "the stone" in an age when the computer and direct imputting were still unknown.

Bill Myles, who had been my Editor on *The Tipperary Star*, had groomed me well for the role of Editorship. His great operating dictum when it came to avoiding libel was: "When in doubt, leave it out". As a man who had been an officer of the Irish Free State Army in the Civil War and who knew Dan Breen well (Breen was sickened really at the thought of a Civil War and had no stomach for it), Bill Myles was magnificent when it came to instructing us on how to write the obituary of those who had been out in "The Troubles".

If someone was a real hero, he got the full treatment. But if there was a question-mark over what some supposed diehard had claimed he achieved, Myles would tell me to use the term "identified with The Cause". Everyone in County Tipperary knew the coded language (like the language of the Diplomatic world) and it could be very cruel on anyone who had lined his pockets under the guise of setting out to die for Ireland.

*A selection of my pictures formed* The Nationalist *display at the Clonmel Horse Show.*

Sadly, *The Munster Tribune* was already on the slippery slope to extinction when I joined the paper on a six-month contract. Nick Strappe of The Mick Delahunty Story fame and the late Mick Hogan and myself worked ourselves to the bone to try and keep the ship afloat in stormy economic seas. But the truth of the matter was that *The Tribune* could never take the auction advertisements from *The Nationalist* and could not break the powerbase of *The Star* in Thurles or that of *The Guardian* in Nenagh. Perhaps, it was a case that four papers could not be accommodated in the one county, especially when you reflect that the North had one, the Mid had one and the South had one already.

I had joined *Independent Newspapers* in the Spring of 1960 when *The Munster Tribune* was bought out by *The Nationalist*. But as Scott Fitzgerald might put it, the south sings for me with a sense of nostalgia for those happy times past whenever I hit Clonmel nowadays. It was a brief sojourn really, almost a passing through for me, as it was for the others who moved on to different pastures.

But there is a memory of coursing days with frost in the air and camaraderie all about me - of travelling with bookmaker and born character, Patsy Browne to Kilkenny, where a few years earlier I had the unique privilege of seeing, and writing about, the immortal Prairie Champion, later to win the English Derby at the White City as Pigalle Wonder . . . of friendships forged with "doggy" men of the calibre of John Fielding of Thurles, Paddy Dunphy of Castlecomer and the Nugents of Clonmel and of working with Johnny Morrissey, Jim Murphy and Paddy Fitzgerald, three men with ourstanding knowledge.

Yes, it was an era all its own.

OPPOSITE PAGE: *The Presentation Convent Leaving Cert. class.*

ABOVE: *Claire Roche presents the Roche Trophy at the Island Tennis Club.*

RIGHT: *The farm staff at Knocklofty gathered to make a retirement presentation to Mr. Bovenizer on his retirement.*

ABOVE RIGHT: *Catherine Slattery from Irishtown.*

ABOVE: *Singers Paddy Hickey and Alice McCormack who took part in the "Factory Frolics" in the Regal as did the three ladies on left.*

TOP LEFT: There were clubs catering for every sport - including pigeon racing.

LEFT: Golf Club winners - while (above) is another golf group from Bulmers and Smithwicks who came together for an outing.

LEFT: Members of the Red Cross who held their social at Ferryhouse.

BELOW: The brainy ones! They received their certificates in the Tech.

LEFT: The organising committee of the South Tipperary County Council Social held in the Courthouse.

During the 'fifties the Mayoral election was quite a lively occasion with the winner's name in some doubt right up to the casting of votes.

However (below right) Martin Cronin and Matt Slater did not allow Party affiliations interfere with their friendship.

Afterwards, we would all go off and enjoy the Mayoral Banquet!

OPPOSITE PAGE: *Despite reports of harsh regimes in some institutions in the 1950's, there is no doubting the happiness of these boys who were well cared for by the Rosminian Order at Ferryhouse.*

ABOVE: *Although they had gathered to climb Galtee Mór their footwear seems particularly unsuited for the task.*

TOP RIGHT: *Lady members of Clonmel Golf Club.*

RIGHT: *They took part in a tennis tournament in Cahir Park.*

RIGHT: Before the jet age the propellor Constellations lumbered slowly across the Atlantic - in this case bringing Tipperary exiles home to a Shannon Airport still under construction.

BELOW: Mick Kelly, who was an insurance agent with New Ireland, called to all of us in the newspaper office each week collecting a few shillings on life policies. Here he is with Mrs. Kelly on the occasion of their daughter's First Holy Communion.

BELOW RIGHT: Irish dance troupe at a Céilí in the Casino.

Party time at the Casino.

*Soon after joining* The Nationalist *one of my earliest assignments was to visit the* Mitchelstown Caves *with* **Peggie Hickey**. *In those days the descent of almost a mile into the ground was quite scary with the only light coming from a Tilly oil lamp (as seen in the accompanying photo being carried here by the guide Kathleen Mulcahy). Later when Jackie English married Kathleen he installed spectacular lighting and carried out massive renovations to the entrance, making ready access for the thousands of tourists who now visit the spectacular caves. 35 years later, I returned to make TV history by producing an entire* Bibi Show *half a mile underground and featured a wide variety of artistes in the programme, including the St. Mary's Choral Society. The photo shows Kathleen, Peggie and myself in 1956, with inset Bibi as she appeared in the underground "studio" on the occasion of the TV broadcast.*

*Here Peggie writes her:*

# Recollections of a Happy Era

"My connection with The Nationalist began in 1955, at about the same time as Justin Nelson joined the paper. Prior to this, I had been contributing short weekly articles, but when the Editor, Mr. William Darmody, phoned me with the offer of a permanent job it literally transformed my life. With delight I accepted - for it finally closed the door on many years of serious illness from tuberculosis - which at that time sped through the country taking many lives. My spine was affected, causing paralysis, and the outlook was very bleak indeed. However, thanks to the prayers of my family and friends, the surgical skills of the late Mr. Robert O'Driscoll, as well as new advances in medication, I made a wonderful recovery.

Lying in my spinal contraption, I became an avid reader and then found I had the urge to write - first poetry and then short stories.

These were regularly published in various magazines, and I frequently won prizes for poetry in the *Cork Weekly Examiner*. I bought a tiny typewriter with the proceeds, and my father, gifted with his hands, made an ingenious desk from plywood which allowed me type quite comfortably while lying down. This activity took place at home in the garden, between spells in hospital for additional surgery. I lived in a timber chalet which opened into a veranda by day, built by Tommy Stapleton of Davis Terrace. At that time he was with the building firm of Roche, Morrissey and Kennedy, but later went to find his true forte as a woodworker instructor in Callan Vocational School. He now lives in retirement with his wife Babs.

And so it came about that I began writing weekly articles for *The Nationalist*, in which I presented a pen picture of a particular place or beauty spot designed to recall a happy memory for the emigrant. Mr. Darmody, who always came up with the most apt headings, called the series *"Clonmel Cameo"*. It was to be the paving stone to better things. Another newcomer, Willie Fenton joined the paper at the same time, and one of his specialities was the very popular column *"Down Memory Lane"*.

My duties also included proof reading, which was interesting in that it gave me a knowledge of every item printed in the paper, including the advertising. While I corrected the "proofs" looking out for mis-spelt words - (reading aloud incidentally) - another staff member held the original copy to ensure that the "proof" and original copy matched. Eventually this work was taken over by the printing department.

Starting the paper's first *Woman's Column*, I quickly realised that the shops were a great source of interest, as all kinds of goods began to arrive after the shortages of the previous decade when World War 2 raged through Europe. Household gadgets provided a wealth of interesting material for my column. Lowrey's Ironmongers at the corner of Gladstone St. and Market St. (see photo right) - now occupied by the ACC offices was a treasure trove in this line. The manager, Tom Tobin, always kept me informed of new arrivals; such as a fire shovel with long slits which was ideal for riddling the cinders when cleaning the fireplace, and a carrot peeler which had come on the market for the first time.

Surprisingly in the midst of all the nails, hammers and tools, Lowrey's also had a wool section presided over by Siddon Dwan who later married Dick Bolger, a clerk in the Post Office (also seen in photo on right) just up the street opposite SS. Peter & Paul's Church, which is now a book shop and restaurant.

*In those days the paper carried advertising on its front page with the main news pages well illustrated.*

In the mid-50s, Clonmel had its first Fashion shows, introduced by Ryan's Exhibition House which was beside the Oisin Cinema in O'Connell St. The first of these shows took place in the shop, and so many people attended that it had to be held twice in the same night. The Exhibition House was renowned for it' original and artistic window displays, arranged by Mrs Lily Ryan herself. She could, by a few delicate touches, convey a seasonal atmosphere as she specialised in nature studies.

For their next show, Ryan's chose the Municipal Theatre on the Mall as their venue, and once again there was a capacity audience, mainly women. The collection was shown by models from the Betty Whelan Agency and also by Mr. and Mrs Ryan's daughter Eleanor (in centre of above group). A feature of this first major fashion show was the long, high carpeted dais which ran from the stage half way down the aisle. Appropriate music was played on the Hammond Organ by Zavier Gibson with commentary by William Begley of Alan Gay's in Dublin.

*Betty Whelan and her models were received by Mayor Jim Taylor at the Town Hall.*

On another such occasion in the Municipal Theatre, one of the models making a guest appearance was a Beauty Queen winner from the U.K. She may well have been the "Miss World" of that year - but certainly Justin needed no coaxing in order to ask her to pose for his camera! (see photo on right).

And now to footwear fashions. In the Summer of 1956 Munster Shoes - or the Boot Factory as it was known, presented its Autumn range of ladies and children's footwear, which was also launched with great success in London, Leicester, Scotland and Northern Ireland. The sales manager, Sean Hogan, had special praise for the designer, a young Clonmel man Paddy O'Shea, who is nowadays recognised as a gifted landscape painter. Munster Shoes unfortunately did not survive.

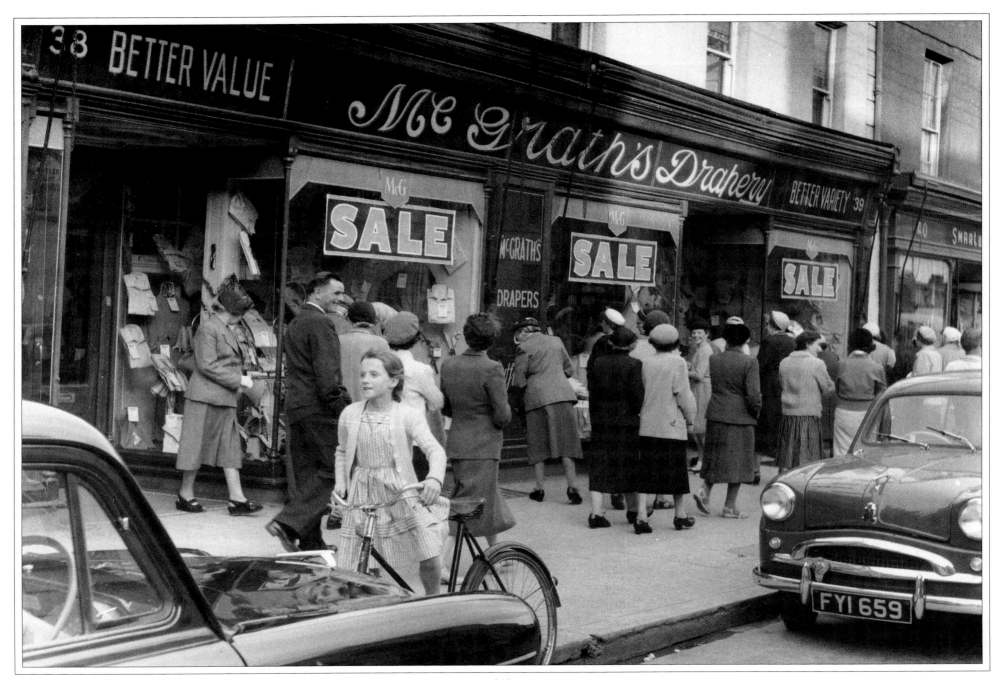

Clonmel is now a swiftly changing town, with many of the shops we knew and loved gone from the scene (such as McGrath's in Gladstone Street - see opposite page) and replaced by new buildings. There are even gaps where there was once a well known shop or business. For instance Miss Belynda Cashin's Music Salon opposite the Friary, which is now a car park .

Mr. Tom McGrath lived in the adjoining house, while a little further down towards the river a large gate (shown in photo on right) led into the Friary garden where the late Fr. Fabian used to tend bees - an activity which was born when a swarm descended on the garden.

Belynda Cashin at home.

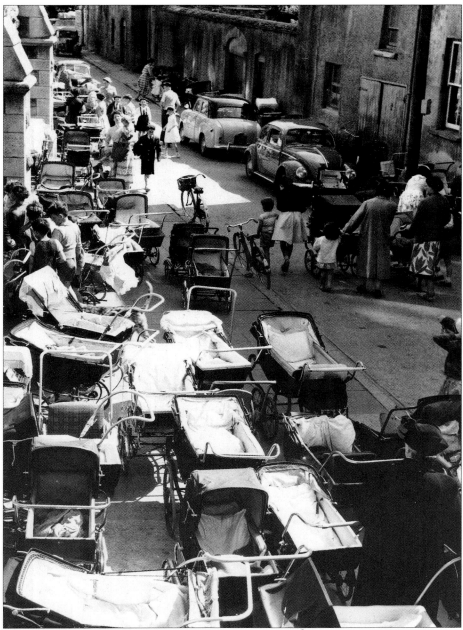

This pram-jam outside of the Friary resulted when the mothers took their babies in to a St. Anthony's Novena.

211

Miss Cashin's frequent advertisments in *The Nationalist* bore the heading - "*Think of it!*" adding that her salon was noted as being "*The House of Distinction*" for gramophones - electric and otherwise, records, radios, pianos, violins. A lady of buxom build, Miss Cashin's rather brusque manner hid a heart of gold. She took a special interest in aspiring young musicians such as the group below who were winners of a piano competition held in the Regal. Mary Hackett (above right) was also a talented singer and had her trophy to prove it.

Her brother Tom had a large drapery business in O'Connell Street beside Quirk's Pharmacy, where quite a number of local girls were

employed. Tom was a kindly man with a twinkling sense of humour. A new furniture store now occupies the site.

Across the road where Heaton's now stands, we had the Oisin Theatre (see page nine), where, besides films, we enjoyed Jimmy O'Dea's and Frank O'Donovan's variety shows, as well as many local concerts, as Edmond Symes describes elsewhere in this book. How devastated we all were when it was burned down one stormy night.

Another popular rendezvous for music lovers was Mr. Christy O'Riordan's music shop at 15 Irishtown, which is now an Antique Shop. (See photo of Christy with the Mick Del. Band on extreme right of the photo on page 58). An advertisement of Christy's from the 'fifties indicates the musical tastes of the period - Paul Robeson's L.P.; songs from the Scottish tenor, Father Sydney McEwan; Victor Sylvester numbers, and Christmas Carols by Harry Belafonte.

Dunne's Stores in O'Connell Street was formerly the site of Mr. and Mrs. J.P. Brady's large store which specialised in bicycles, prams, and musical goods among other things. "*Bradyo for Radio*" was a great slogan of the firm, and in advertising in *The Nationalist*. Mr. Brady often used a photograph of himself looking very debonair strolling along the promenade in, I think, the Isle of Man. Brady's is still going strong in O'Connell Street, mainly specialising in the television and radio business, and situated on the opposite side of the street.

RIGHT: *Brady's Shop in O'Connell Street as it was in the 1950's.*

ABOVE: *This group photographed at a Hillview Ball includes two of the Brady girls, while another, Mona, married Senator Des Hanafin (see page 57).*

ABOVE RIGHT: *The opening of the new Provincial Bank Premises in O'Connell Street.*

We don't nowadays have a milliner in Clonmel, but in the late 'fifties Mrs. Dempsey was practising her craft in the building which is now "Eileen's" in Mitchel Street; and had been there for many years. I wrote at the time that her little workroom had been the sanctum of numerous women with hat problems, not to mention the hundreds of brides-to-be.

Mrs. Dempsey, who came to Clonmel from Killarney, was, before establishing her own business, with the renowned fashion house of A. & J. Hanna, Parnell Street, Clonmel - now Clintons. At that time the trend was for high-crowned, forehead-covering hats! And what have we today? The circle certainly keeps turning.

Also in Mitchel Street, the brothers Eddie and Michael Dillon had a tailoring establishment, and were renowned for their craftsmanship. They were uncles of the late Ted of *The Nationalist* editorial staff. Their sister was the wife of Mr. David Stapleton who had a very select grocery business on the opposite side of the street. This is now Barrett's Drapery.

In the Spring of 1958, Esther Hackett, daughter of Mr. and Mrs. A. Hackett, Morton Street, Clonmel, was selected from hundreds of applicants to train as Trans World Airlines Hostess in Kansas City, U.S.A. Prior to emigrating, Esther was a popular clerk at Wall's Turf Accountancy office in Gladstone Street. The following June, having successfully completed the prescribed training, she was awarded her wings.

LEFT: *Delany's Shop at the corner of O'Connell Street and Gladstone Street is no longer there. It was formerly O'Reilly's where the sign on the wall advertised Irish tweed suits made to measure for 30 shillings or £1.50.*

The Town Hall and the adjoining Cantwell's Jewellers as it looked before the recent renovations were carried out.

Clonmel's Town Hall in Parnell Street was completely renovated in recent years, and the adjoining premises, formerly Messrs. Cantwell, Jewellers, incorporated into the structure. The late Miss May Lonergan, who had a greengrocery in O'Connell Street, and was excellent in tracing the history of the various street premises, said that the Town Hall was formerly the Great Globe Hotel. But she could go back further into history when it was Hamerton Hall. To quote her words on the subject:

"Hamerton Hall, the residence of the Hamertons of Orchardstown - the famous General Hamerton was a son of theirs. They had a big notice outside: 'Welcome all to the Hamerton Hall' and they fed the poor of the town and country. They were very wealthy and very charitable."

She added that the last member of the family, Miss Hamerton, who died in the 'sixties, lived at "Auburn", William Street, Clonmel. She also recalled that a gate between the Town Hall and Mrs. Cantwell's, jewellers, was "the old lock-up where prisoners were lodged before being sentenced".

Many of the young step-dancers of the 'fifties in Clonmel (like the group above right) wore Irish linen dance costumes, richly embroidered in Celtic designs. So very beautiful, they bore the mark of distinction. Whenever I asked the name of the magic-fingered needlewoman, I was invariably told - "Mrs Lyons of Árd-na-Greine". A gentle, motherly woman, Mrs Frances Lyons lived in a bungalow-style house on the crest of a high slope facing the Comeragh foothills. In this lovely setting she carried on a tiny industry.

Her interest in needlecraft stemmed from her schooldays, when she was taught scientific pattern-cutting by the Sisters of Charity at their schools in Morton Street. Later she attended night classes at Clonmel Technical School, where she studied drawing and painting under the direction of Mr. Golden, and later, Mr. R.J. Long, father of Brendan Long. This laid the foundation for her embroidery - she traced her own designs on the linen. Mrs. Lyons handed on her expertise to her daughter, Mrs. Bessie Hogg, and the gift was also inherited by one of her grand-daughters, Iris. Both Mrs. Lyons and Mrs. Hogg have since passed to their eternal reward.

THE CEANN COMHAIRLE (pictured at SS. Peter & Paul's Church on his wedding day)

"I always had a flair for chairmanship, and I feel now that I may have found my forte," This gift of Mr. Sean Treacy's was nurtured at a social Science course in Clonmel in the 'fifties. Who could foresee then that it would eventually lead him to the office of Ceann Comhairle and Chairmanship of the National Assembly, the fourth highest position in the land after the President, Taoiseach, and the Chief Justice.

The course was under the direction of the late Professor Alfred O'Rahilly of Cork University, and the other students elected Sean Treacy as chairman of their group.

Following his successful graduation he was well prepared to take over the Mayoralty of Clonmel on two occasions - in the periods '58/'59 and '60/'61; and the chairmanship of South Tipperary County Council on two occasions also.

To Mr. Treacy the advent of the Social Science course was a tremendous opportunity of supplementing his education. He is the second eldest boy of a family of three sisters and four brothers.

The Ceann Comhairle came from a very old-established Clonmel family. John Treacy, his grandfather, owned a public-house and posting establishment (with the contract for the mail cars for this area) and a funeral and undertaking business at the corner of Irishtown and O'Neill Street. When his parents, Mr. and Mrs. James Treacy got married they moved into another licensed premises on the Irishtown side of West Gate. Later they moved to Mary Street where Sean was born.

# Epilogue

It seems like only yesterday when first I came to Clonmel. Yet it is now an unbelievable 40 years. The publication of the first edition of my photographic memories of the '50s gave me great enjoyment while assembling the images of those golden days. However, it was nothing when compared to the pleasure I got from returning to this town I love so well and being greeted so warmly by my loyal friends from that era at the book launch just a few short weeks ago.

Clonmel means so much to me that I was prepared to carry the substantial cost of the book's publication myself. However, the immediate success of the venture in terms of sales  has been an unexpected bonus, and I can now see the prospects of recovering my initial outlay with the printing of this second edition within such a short time of its initial launch by the Ceann Comhairle Sean Treacy T.D. and Ald. Tom Ambrose, Mayor of Clonmel. (See photo on opposite page where they are pictured with Sean Boland, Managing Director of *The Nationalist* at the launch in Hearn's Hotel). Their enthusiastic endorsement of my efforts, together with their most flattering comments has been a major help in creating interest in the publication.

In addition to all the old friends that I met during my book signing sessions of that first edition, there are many others for whom I hold fond memories and I hope that they too will have an opportunity to view these pages. My hope is that readers both at home and abroad will enjoy this trip down memory lane.

During my years in Clonmel, I often heard people refer to a book from the turn of the century called "My Clonmel Scrapbook". My wish is that copies of this book too will survive in the homes of Tipperary, so that future generations can take this volume down from the bookshelves to relive the times of their forefathers in this valley near Slievenamon.

For this is My Clonmel Snapbook. I hope you have enjoyed its pages.

*Justin Nelson*

June 1996